Bake Me a Cat

50
Purrrfect Recipes
for Edible Kitty Cakes,
Cookies and More!

Kim-Joy

PHOTOGRAPHY BY ELLIS PARRINDER
ILLUSTRATIONS BY LINDA VAN DEN BERG
LETTERING DESIGN BY MARY KATE McDEVITT

Hardie Grant

QUADRILLE

Contents

Introduction

This book is a celebration of my love for two of the most joyous things in this world: cats and baking. We all know that cats are cute, calming and quirky. And baking is also cute, calming… and full of its own quirks and joys. The two already have a lot in common, so put them together and you have the most epic power duo resulting in adorable (and tasty) creations, such as cosy cats in fruit tarts, kitties on the beach cake, psychedelic cat pop tarts and even grumpy ginger snap cats!

My aim is for every recipe to guide you smoothly through the baking process like a warm kitten cuddle, providing lots of tips and advice throughout – and, at the same time, to help you tap into your own creativity and ideas. My hope is that you'll end up staring at your croissant at breakfast, thinking about whether – and how – it could look like a cat. Once you learn the techniques on pages 8–25, you will have all the tools you need to make any bake cat-themed – so that may well happen!

I also want to ensure that there is something here for everyone, whether you're completely new to baking or already an experienced baker. I've given each recipe a Paw Rating to indicate its general difficulty, 1 paw being the easiest, and 5 paws being the hardest. This is a good initial guide (especially if you're working with small children!), but it is subjective depending on what plays to your strengths! If something is 4 paws but you feel confident enough to try, then go for it.

There are also clearly marked vegan and/or gluten-free substitutions, only included when I think they're just as good! It's important to me that not only do the bakes look cute, but that they (first and foremost) taste good. So, even if your decorating doesn't look how you imagined, it ultimately doesn't matter: it's about the relaxing process of baking, and then getting to eat something delicious at the end.

Luckily, when it comes to decorating, there's one big advantage to having cats as your muse: they are all unique and individual creatures. Maybe your piped cat face looks a bit spooked – but don't cats pull faces like that sometimes? Maybe your marshmeowllow cat is flat and round – well, that's charming and accurately cat-like, isn't it? It's all intentional, right?

This leads me to the most important message I want you to take away from this book – to embrace the quirkiness and joy of cats and express this through your baking, and life. Cats are loved for their weird behaviour, like sleeping in bizarre positions, tongue bleps and staring blankly. It's the same with baking: the weirder and less uniform the decoration, the more loved it will be. Have fun with it. Make 'mistakes'. Focus on enjoying the process, not on how it turns out.

Think more like a cat. Would a cat worry about overbaking a pie? Probably not.

Would a cat bake a cake in their own likeness and be the proudest ever? Well, probably not as they can't really bake, but they would certainly be the proudest ever (of anything they did).

BAKE AND BE PROUD LIKE A CAT!

Kim-Joy
And Inki and Mochi (my two cats and big inspirations)

I share baking videos and advice on my Instagram and YouTube @kimjoy. I'm also on TikTok @kimjoyskitchen.

How to use this book

BUTTER
This refers to butter that is close to or around 80% fat content, not margarine.

Many recipes state salted butter for ease, but you can substitute this with unsalted butter and add a little salt to taste.

GLUTEN-FREE
All the substitutions are based on using a gluten-free plain flour blend, or gluten-free self-raising flour blend. It's crucial to use a blend of different gluten-free flours for the recipes to work, not just a single gluten-free flour. I use Doves Farm Freeee flour, which blends rice, potato, tapioca, maize and buckwheat.

Xanthan gum is necessary when specified, as it helps to bind and improves mouth feel. The gluten-free plain flour blend I use doesn't contain any xanthan gum, so it needs to be added to different recipes in the specified quantities. Some gluten-free flour blends will already include a little xanthan gum, but different additional amounts are required in different bakes depending on how much binding is needed (pastry and cookies often need a little more than cakes). The gluten-free self-raising flour blend I use (also Doves Farm!) does contain some xanthan gum, but a little extra is often required, and again the amount is specified in the recipes.

Make sure that you buy a gluten-free baking powder, as not all are gluten-free.

SIFTING
Some recipes will specifically state that you need to sift certain ingredients. If this isn't stated, but your flour/cocoa powder/icing sugar (or any dry ingredient) appears lumpy from being left to sit around or being exposed to moisture, then do sift this before incorporating it into the mixture to make mixing easier for yourself.

OVENS
All recipes are based on a fan-assisted [convection] oven. If your oven is not fan-assisted, raise the temperature by 10–20°C.

Ovens can vary a little and may reach a different temperature to the one you set it to, or it might have hot and cool spots – you know your oven best so adjust the timings if necessary.

CHILLING
Many recipes state that you can place mixtures in either the fridge or the freezer prior to baking. The choice is yours – it will depend on the space you have in your fridge/freezer and how much time you have! Just note that some cookies won't brown as much if they've been chilled for longer in the freezer, but will still taste the same.

I often prefer to chill shortbread-style cookies in the freezer. This ensures that they're fully chilled, so won't spread during baking and will keep a nice pale colour.

STORING BAKES
Ideally, store all bakes in a cool dark place, and in an airtight container – though plastic wrap will work in a pinch! The fridge will dry out most bakes so avoid refrigerating, unless the bake contains fresh cream and must be kept in the fridge.

If baking cake layers in advance, you can wrap the layers tightly in plastic wrap, once baked, and freeze them to keep the cake layers moist and fresh. Just let them defrost slightly before decorating. Most cookie and pastry doughs can be shaped and then kept in the freezer before baking.

VANILLA BEAN PASTE
I prefer to flavour with vanilla bean paste rather than vanilla extract, because vanilla bean paste has great depth of

flavour, and you will be able to see the real vanilla bean flecks. Ultimately though, either is fine and you can substitute with an equal amount of vanilla extract. Just bear in mind that the extract is thinner than vanilla bean paste and can therefore have a minor impact on the consistency of things like buttercreams.

FOOD DYES

I like to use gel food dyes, but note that not all gel food dyes are made equal. It really helps to buy good-quality ones, particularly if baking in the oven, as some poor-quality food dyes do not bake up very vibrantly. Brands I like to use include Americolor, Coloursplash, Colourmill and Rainbow Dust ProGel.

Most gel food dyes are water-based, which combine well in most water- or low-fat-based mixtures. But for buttercreams (particularly Italian meringue buttercream) and high-fat cake mixtures, an oil-based food dye will mix much better, producing more vibrant results.

Pure melted chocolate must be coloured with oil-based food dye, as a small drop of a water-based food dye will cause it to seize and become unworkable.

VEGAN SUBSTITUTIONS

When substituting vegan butter, this should be in block form and have a fat content of around 75–80% for best results. A lower fat content means a higher water content, and this will change the end result. It's especially important to keep the fat content high for recipes like pastry or cookies.

I like using the Naturli vegan butter block, which is 75% fat and works well in all recipes.

Any plant-based milk will work in all the recipes in this book, but ideally avoid using low-fat or reduced-fat plant milks.

Most regular white sugar brands in the UK are vegan, but in the US and other countries, check that it isn't filtered using bone char, which would make it not vegan. You should also check that the icing sugar you're using is vegan, as some brands add dried egg whites.

BREADS

The time for bread dough to rise can vary dramatically based on the ambient temperature of where it's placed. So dough will rise in the fridge – just very slowly! In contrast, it will rise very rapidly once it's around body temperature.

If you're in a rush and wanting it to rise quickly, leave it somewhere warm or put the oven on very low and place it in there. Make sure to cover the dough with oiled plastic wrap to prevent it from forming a skin. You will notice that with some doughs, it doesn't look like much is happening for a while, but once the internal temperature of the dough gets warm enough, it might suddenly start to quickly expand! Generally though, longer and colder rises result in more flavoursome dough, so it's better to take your time, if you can!

PAW DIFFICULTY

These ratings refer to the difficulty of the recipe – the more paws, the more skill is required! These ratings are just an initial guide, but there's always subjectivity depending on your strengths as a baker. For instance, *Meowringues* (page 16) are labelled as 4 paws (❀ ❀ ❀ ❀), but you might be a master meringue maker, in which case trust your skills. Just like a cat, you and only you know what's best for you!

❀ kitten mode
❀ ❀ ❀ house cat mode
❀ ❀ ❀ ❀ ❀ boss cat mode

Cat Basics

How to add kitty cuteness to any bake

Anything you bake – whether it be a simple cake, a tray of doughnuts, a stack of pancakes, a crème brûlée, a pile of croissants – litter-ally ANYTHING – can be elevated to maximum kitten cuteness with the addition of any one of these easy, simple techniques or with any of the edible 3D cats in this section.

You have a choice of cats in the form of 3D cookies, marshmeowllows, meowringues, buttercream, fondant or marzipan. And each recipe section shows you the main shapes and tips that work best with each medium of baking, keeping the shape as simple and uncomplicated as possible for fast cat creating – but still with meowximum impact. You can stick to the ideas shown here, or you can totally go off in your own direction with colours, different expressions and your own cute accessories. There are so many ways to do it, so get your thinking cat on!

Many of these techniques and recipes are stand-alone creations, so you can happily serve a plate of 3D Cookie Cats (page 12) all piled up, if you like, but even more magic happens when you claw-verly add these cats to finished bakes from the other sections of this book. You can have a sleepy kitten cosying up in your fruit tart (page 108), a kitty wrapped in your cake roll as a 'purrito' (page 51) or you might have a greedy chonky cat gobbling your very own cake (page 62). You can even use these in your everyday store-bought or homemade bakes… because every bake without a cute cat is a missed oppawtunity!

CAT TIP To make these Scruffy Meowringue Cats, make the Meowringue recipe on page 17, but instead of transferring the mixture into piping bags, use a teaspoon to dollop it onto a baking sheet lined with baking paper instead. Spoon some more meringue on top of each dollop for the head, then use the spoon to create texture and swirl through different flavours, if you like. Try biscoff spread, chocolate spread, curd (page 72), jam and freeze-dried fruits. Then pinch the meringue heads with your fingers to create two pointed ears and use your fingers or a fork to create more texture. You can dab some more meringue on for the tail too. Bake following the instructions on page 17. Paint a face using black food dye mixed with a tiny amount of water, or pipe on with Quick Black Icing (page 12). **DIFFICULTY** ❀ ❀

3D Cookie Cats

These are German-style cookies, which have a unique melt-in-your-mouth texture due to a secret ingredient... potato starch! It might not sound that tasty an ingredient on its own, but put it into a baked cookie and it's a game changer. Feel free to make cats of all shapes, colours and sizes, and don't *fur*-get – the bigger the cat, the longer it will take to bake. This dough is super tactile and therapeutic, both to work with and shape – almost like working with playdough, but edible!

DIFFICULTY 🐾 🐾 The dough is incredibly quick and simple to make, then all you need to do is to shape the kitties. You can make these as simple or as elaborate as you like.

MAKES: AROUND 8 MEDIUM CATS, OR MORE IF YOU MAKE SMALL KITTENS!

Can be made gluten-free and/or vegan

125g [½ cup plus 1 Tbsp] salted butter, at room temperature, cubed (or vegan butter – use one that's close to 80% fat content)
40g [3¼ Tbsp] icing [confectioners'] sugar
½ tsp vanilla bean paste
125g [⅔ cup] potato starch
80g [⅔ cup minus 1 Tbsp] plain [all-purpose] flour (or to make gluten-free, substitute with a gluten-free plain flour blend plus ¾ tsp xanthan gum)
gel food dyes (brown, orange and black help create realistic kitties, but you can also use blues, purples and pinks for *meowgical* cats!)

QUICK BLACK ICING
¾ tsp water
20g [2¼ tsp] icing [confectioners'] sugar
black gel food dye

> **CAT TIP** *"The main thing to purr in mind when baking us is that we are COOKIES, so our butter melts and gravity will take effect while baking. As a general rule to ensure we're feline fine, avoid placing our heads where they might sink backwards with gravity, or our paws in the air as they will sink down! But don't worry too much – unusual and different looking cats are what makes us interesting and funny, so experiment and see where it takes you."*

Continued overleaf

- CAT BASICS -

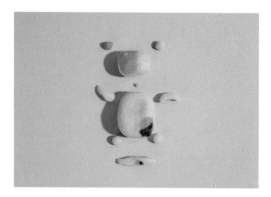

1 / Line a large baking sheet with baking paper.

2 / Add the chopped butter to a large bowl along with the icing sugar. Beat together with a spoon or spatula until smooth and spreadable, then add the vanilla and mix again until combined. Add the potato starch and plain flour (plus xanthan gum, if gluten-free) – sifting if there are any lumps – then use a spoon or spatula to mix into a paste. Avoid overmixing. Use your hands to combine the dough into a ball.

3 / Divide some of the dough into different bowls (depending on how many different colours you want) and use a spoon or your hands to mix in food dye to colour. Using your hands and the pictures above as a guide, shape the dough into 8 cat shapes. Avoid pressing too hard and sticking your fingers too far into the dough if you want to stop it sticking to your hands! You can use a little flour to stop them sticking, but you shouldn't need any if you try to handle the dough lightly.

4 / Place the shaped cats onto the prepared baking sheet and chill in the fridge for at least 40 minutes, or in the freezer for 10 minutes. Meanwhile, preheat the oven to 140°C [275°F/Gas mark 1].

5 / Bake for 20–40 minutes depending on the size of the cats – you can take smaller ones out sooner, but be careful as they're very fragile! They will expand a little in the oven and can crack ever so slightly, but will hold their shape well. You can tell when they are ready as the whites will look lighter in colour, but it's best to give them an extra 5 minutes past that point to ensure they are properly baked in the centre. Once baked, they will be firm enough to pick up without collapsing – gently transfer to a wire rack and leave to cool.

6 / After the cookies have cooled, you can give the kitties their facial features using quick black icing. To make this, whisk the water and icing sugar together in a small bowl until smooth, then add black food

dye to colour. You may need to add a tiny bit more icing sugar or water to adjust the consistency so that it's suitable for piping. You are looking for an icing that holds a trail for 15–20 seconds, then goes smooth and flat.

7 / Transfer the icing to a piping [pastry] bag and cut a very small tip. Use this to pipe on eyes, whiskers and mouth details. There are so many different ways to decorate these – you can even create different icing colours and pipe on cute accessories, or make quirky accessories from fondant! Store in an airtight container for up to 1 week.

Fondant Cats

Sometimes, you may just want some quick fondant cats. The advantage of working with fondant, compared to other mediums, is that these cats are sturdy and easily mouldable, and you don't need to worry so much about the baking process changing the end result. The cat you shape and see is instantly what you get! There are limitless ways to create unique cats with fondant (and you can even use marzipan or modelling chocolate if you like!).

DIFFICULTY 🐾 🐾 The basic shaping is similar to the 3D Cookie Cats opposite – the key differences being that the fondant holds up better to gravity, so there is greater range in what shapes are possible, and you can paint fondant much more easily. You have the option to paint the face on using food dye mixed with a little water, and you can paint the cats to give them markings or even watercolour patches. Follow the step-by-step pictures to get an idea of the basic shape, and then you can create variations using similar building blocks (see pages 28 or 51 for ideas!).

STEP 1 ▼

STEP 2 ▼

STEP 3 ▼

STEP 4 ▼

- CAT BASICS -

Meowringues

The combination of using icing [confectioners'] sugar and heating the mixture ensures that no large grains of sugar remain, as they could easily cause cracks in these finely detailed character meringues. Make sure you whisk at medium-high speed (not maximum) to incorporate less air, as you'll get fewer trapped air bubbles when piping – these can also cause cracks. The step-by-step photos are just one way to do it! See pages 11, 39, 72 or 77 for more shapes you can make. Follow the key steps, get creative, then litter any of your bakes with these adorable meringues to create some *meow-gic!*

DIFFICULTY 🐾 🐾 🐾 🐾
This is a little higher due to the careful piping needed. If you struggle with piping, try making the equally cute variation on page 11.

MAKES: 1 LARGE TRAY OF MERINGUES

Naturally gluten-free and can be made vegan

130g [4½oz] egg white (from about 4 medium eggs) (or use aquafaba – reduce this down first following the instructions on page 118)
260g [2 cups minus 2 Tbsp] icing [confectioners'] sugar
1 tsp vanilla bean paste

PLUS

gel food dyes (colours depend on which cat designs you are making)
edible black ink pen or black food dye mixed with a little water

CAT TIP *So that you don't waste any eggs, weigh the egg whites, then use double the amount of icing sugar to however much egg white you have. Reserve the egg yolks to make a delicious Lemon Curd (page 72).*

1 / Preheat the oven to 80°C [176°F/Gas mark ¼]. Line 2 baking sheets with baking paper or silicone mats.

2 / Add the egg white and icing sugar to a large, clean bowl. Whisk using a handheld electric whisk (or use a stand mixer fitted with a balloon whisk attachment) until combined.

3 / Place the bowl over a pan of boiling water (don't let the the bowl touch the water!) and whisk for about 10 minutes, or until the sugar has dissolved. Remove from the heat.

4 / Using a handheld electric whisk or stand mixer, whisk on medium-high speed until the mixture is foamy. Add the vanilla, reduce the speed to medium and whisk for 10 minutes, or until the mixture is bright white, glossy and has stiff peaks (they should stand straight up – no flopping over!).

5 / Divide the meringue into different bowls and colour as desired, then transfer to piping [pastry] bags, putting smaller amounts in piping bags for the arms, legs, ears and tail, and larger amounts for the main body and head.

6 / Pipe main body shapes onto the prepared baking sheets using the large piping bag.

7 / Pipe on the smaller details using the smaller piping bags.

8 / To remove the peaks, push them down gently with a damp fingertip.

9 / You can also pipe the faces, along with any very small details now, if you're feeling confident.

10 / Bake for 1 hour 30 minutes, then switch off the oven and leave the meringues inside to cool. Add any remaining facial details using an edible black ink pen or black food dye mixed with a little water. Store in an airtight container for up to 3 weeks.

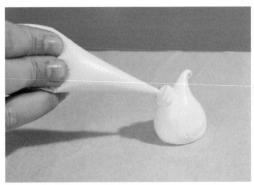

"It's OK if you do get some cracks though – I'll still be cute."

- CAT BASICS -

Squishy Marshmeowllow Cats

These are super squishy, pillowy and utterly delightful. Kids will love floating them in their hot chocolates.

Make sure you're properly prepawed for this – marshmallow is messy and sticky, but it's worth it. It's much easier if you have a stand mixer, but you will be able to manage with a handheld electric whisk and a bit of patience, too. You will also need a thermometer. The good thing is there's no actual baking involved, and once you've got the technique, you'll be able to try out different shaped kitties and make these again and again. You can make all sorts with this pipe-able marshmallow recipe: a cute chonky cat, ghost cat, a cat to float in hot chocolate, a s'mores cat (page 2) and more...

DIFFICULTY 🐾 🐾 🐾 🐾 🐾

Making marshmallow isn't the easiest! If you know you struggle with piping or if you're in a rush, you can also cut indents into store-bought marshmallows to create ear shapes either side, then draw on faces with black food dye mixed with a small amount of water. If you're making these for the Secret Kitten Hot Chocolate Bombe Surprise (page 93) then pipe a face on using marshmallow. To do this, melt a store-bought marshmallow in the microwave for just 1–3 seconds at a time (otherwise it can become VERY hot and bubbly!), then stir in black food dye to colour. Transfer to a piping [pastry] bag and pipe on a simple face.

MAKES: 2 TRAYS' WORTH OF CATS

Naturally gluten-free

neutral-tasting oil, for oiling
60g [⅓ cup] icing [confectioners'] sugar
60g [⅔ cup] cornflour [cornstarch]
110ml [½ cup minus 1 Tbsp] water
3 tsp powdered gelatine
170g [¾ cup plus 1½ Tbsp] caster or granulated sugar

140g [⅔ cup] liquid glucose or corn syrup
pinch of salt
1 tsp vanilla bean paste

PLUS
edible black ink pen or black food dye mixed with a small amount of water

Continued overleaf

- CAT BASICS -

19

1 / Oil 2 large baking sheets. Mix the icing sugar and cornflour together in a bowl, then sift two-thirds of the mixture over the oiled sheets. You want everything to be evenly and generously coated to ensure the marshmallows don't stick. Set aside the remaining mixture for later.

2 / Now, make the marshmallows. Add half the water to a stand mixer bowl (or use a handheld electric whisk – be patient, though, because you'll be whisking for quite a while!), then sprinkle over the gelatine.

3 / Add the remaining water, the caster sugar, liquid glucose and salt to a small saucepan (avoid getting sugar stuck to the sides) and heat over a high heat, without stirring, until the mixture reaches 116°C [241°F]. At this point, put the mixer on low speed, then quickly pour the sugar syrup in. Add the vanilla bean paste, then increase the speed to high and whisk for 5–10 minutes until the mixture is thick, fluffy and pipeable.

4 / Transfer around a fifth of the white mixture to a small piping [pastry] bag and cut a small tip, then transfer the remaining mixture over a few medium piping bags, and cut a large tip on all of these.

5 / See the step-by-step pictures, opposite, showing how to pipe a marshmallow cat onto the prepared baking sheets. Use wet or oiled sharp scissors to cut the mixture after piping (otherwise it will continue to endlessly stretch!). Use the smaller white piping bag to add the ears, tail, etc.

Tip: If your marshmallow is too thick and difficult to pipe, just microwave the whole piping bag in short 1–3-second bursts (yes, no longer than that! The gelatine melts quickly and will bubble, expand and become very hot if overheated), then massage the whole bag to ensure that hot spots are evenly mixed in. Be careful to keep the marshmallow still relatively thick, otherwise it won't hold its shape after piping. If your marshmallow becomes too liquid, just leave it to cool again. You can repeat the heating/cooling as many times as you need.

6 / Repeat to make a gang of cats, spacing these out well – you don't want to risk them accidentally getting knocked and stuck together! Dust in the remaining cornflour and icing sugar mixture. To finish, draw on the faces using an edible ink pen, or you can paint the faces on using black food dye mixed with a small amount of water. You may need to brush off some of the excess cornflour and icing sugar mix first.

7 / Dust the marshmallows with more icing sugar (or cornflour) and leave to dry on a work surface for 2–4 hours before eating as they are, using to decorate bakes (such as Kitty-kat Cake, page 58, or Secret Kitten Hot Chocolate Bombe Surprise, page 93), putting into mugs of hot chocolate, making s'mores or toasting on a fire (if you can face doing that!). If you want to keep them for longer, store them in an airtight container (otherwise they will continue to dry out and go hard!) separated by baking paper for up to 2 weeks.

CAT TIP *"When you pipe my arms, ears, tail and small details, you will definitely want to make sure that the marshmallow is a little runnier than the consistency used for my body, otherwise it will be too tricky to pipe! If the consistency used for these details is correct, then you won't need to use scissors to cut the marshmallow out of the bag."*

STEP 1 ▼

STEP 2 ▼

STEP 3 ▼

STEP 4 ▼

STEP 5 ▼

STEP 6 ▼

- CAT BASICS -

Buttercream Cats

There are two buttercream recipes to choose from when making your buttercream cats: American or Italian meringue (overleaf). Both have their advantages, so it's just about picking which one suits you!

These step instructions and images are just a starting guide – you can make a range of buttercream cat designs (see left, or pages 36 and 48). These may look fiddly, but it helps to break them down into basic shapes and work one step at a time. There's no need to risk piping directly onto a cake: pipe onto pieces of baking paper and freeze for 15 minutes or until solid – then just peel the cat off the paper and transfer wherever you like! For some cats, like the one that's dropped the carrot (left) you will need to pipe directly onto the cake to follow the edge. But you can choose which cats you're comfortable creating!

STEP 1 ▼

STEP 2 ▼

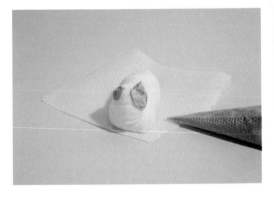
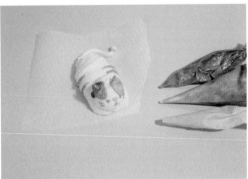

1 / Using a piping [pastry] bag with a large cut opening (or piping tip), pipe an oblong shape for the body (or round if you want a cat sitting up!). Pipe a round blob on top for the head. There may be some buttercream peaks, so just gently tap these down using a finger dipped into a tiny amount of water – a little goes a long way.

2 / Using a piping bag with a small cut opening (or piping tip), add the ears – pipe straight onto the head and pull upwards, gradually reducing pressure on the bag.

3 / Pipe limbs and a tail. It helps to pipe the limbs starting from the paw end, then gradually pulling in towards the body, squeezing less as you go.

4 / Once the basic structure is there, you can also pipe on patches or stripes of colour as you please! If there's any unwanted texture, use the trick of the dampened finger again. If freezing, do this now (see intro), then use a piping bag with a very small opening to add the face details.

Italian Meringue Buttercream

This buttercream is silky, smooth and much less sweet than American buttercream. It's very easy to work with and glides easily on your cakes, but you do need a sugar thermometer and ideally a stand mixer, as you will need to pour in hot sugar syrup while whisking constantly. It takes a little while longer to learn, but once you master the technique, it can be pretty quick to whisk up a batch.

DIFFICULTY 🐾 🐾 🐾

Naturally gluten-free

225g [8oz] egg whites (from about 7–8 medium eggs)
560g [2¾ cups] caster or granulated sugar
¼ tsp salt
225ml [1 cup minus 1 Tbsp] water
½ tsp cream of tartar
600g [2¾ cups] unsalted butter, at room temperature, cubed
1 Tbsp vanilla bean paste or other flavouring
gel food dyes for different coloured buttercream

1 / Place the egg whites in a stand mixer with a balloon whisk attachment. Add half the sugar to a separate bowl.

2 / Place the remaining sugar, salt and the water into a medium pan and mix to make sure that the sugar is hydrated, then heat over a medium-high heat. Don't stir as this will cause the sugar to crystallize.

3 / As soon as the syrup starts bubbling, start whisking the egg whites in the stand mixer. Add the cream of tartar once they are frothy, then when they reach soft peaks, start adding the sugar, 1 Tbsp at a time, until thick and shiny. You will need to time this with the sugar syrup reaching 115°C [239°F]. If necessary, slow down (but don't stop) the mixer or reduce the heat for the sugar syrup. When all the sugar has been added to the meringue and the syrup has reached 115°C

[239°F], pour the syrup down the side of the mixer in a thin stream, mixing on maximum speed. Be careful not to pour the syrup directly onto the whisk, as it's very hot and may splash. Leave to whisk on high speed (to cool the meringue faster) for 30 minutes, or until the bottom of the bowl feels room temperature.

4 / Add the butter, 3–4 cubes at a time, beating well after each addition (ideally, with the paddle mixer attachment, but the whisk attachment will also be fine – it will just incorporate a little more air). Continue until all the butter has been added. The mixture will go from firm to becoming more liquid. This is normal – just keep adding more butter. When you have added all the butter, the mixture will return to being fluffy and the perfect consistency for spreading. At this point you can add your flavouring. Use straight

away, or cover with plastic wrap if using later in the day.

Tip: If the buttercream gets too cold, you will notice it stops being smooth and spreadable. To bring it back to the right consistency, remove about a sixth of the mixture and place in a microwaveable bowl, then microwave for a few seconds until soft. Pour this back into the main bowl of buttercream and stir vigorously with a spatula until the mixture comes back together and looks smooth. If it's still not quite right, repeat the process. It will eventually come together! The buttercream can also be stored in the fridge – just bring it back to room temperature using the microwave method above. If the buttercream looks split and grainy, it is probably too warm. Whisk it vigorously with a balloon whisk to cool it down and it should come back together again.

American Buttercream

American buttercream is the one you will likely be most *fur*-miliar with. Use any electric whisk and simply whisk the butter and sugar together until very light in colour and fluffy. This buttercream is very sweet, quick to make and delicious.

DIFFICULTY ❀ or, if piping, ❀ ❀ ❀

Naturally gluten-free and/or can be made vegan

350g [1½ cups plus 2 tsp] salted butter, at room temperature, cubed (or vegan butter – use one that's close to 80% fat content) OR unsalted butter and fine salt to taste
650g [4⅔ cups] icing [confectioners'] sugar
1 Tbsp vanilla bean paste
2–3 Tbsp milk (or plant-based milk, although you may find you need less milk – or none at all – if using vegan butter, as the buttercream is soft and spreadable enough already)
gel food dyes

1 / Add the butter and icing sugar to a large bowl, then use an electric whisk to beat together for 5–10 minutes. Make sure to keep whisking until it is light, fluffy and very pale in colour. Add the vanilla and whisk again. Then, add the milk to soften the consistency so that it can be easily spread and piped, and finally the gel food dyes.

Note: *These buttercream recipes make a large quantity which can be used to fill, ice [frost] and decorate a large cake with buttercream cats, so you can halve or quarter the quantity if needed. They are both simply flavoured with vanilla bean paste, but you can add and customize the buttercreams with any flavours you like. Try lemon or orange zests, rose water, orange blossom water, freeze-dried fruit, fruit purées, or extracts such as almond, and many more.*

CAT TIPS *"If you're new to making buttercream, then whisk and KEEP whisking for longer than you think it needs until it's definitely no longer becoming fluffier and lighter in colour. It should become noticeably lighter in colour – almost white.*

You can use oil- or water-based food dyes, but oil-based dyes often mix better and produce more vibrant colours for us when we're in buttercream form, due to the high fat content. This is even more noticeable with Italian meringue buttercream than American style."

Cakes

The Roarsome Vi-cat-oria Sponge

I'm not lion when I say that this classic Victoria Sponge is *purrfection*. Light sponge, sweet jam and silky whipped cream; it's always a crowd-pleaser. The traditional method of equal weights of butter, sugar, eggs and flour always works, so the only tweak in my version is that I add a little bit of cornflour [cornstarch] into the mix, which creates an extra tender cake. This cake is made even more fun with the playful cats hanging out in it (and the lion that wishes he was on top of the cake, but has been downgraded to in between the cake layers due to being outnumbered by ordinary house cats).

Tips to ensure this cake is extra tender, light and delicious: Make sure you cream the butter and sugar for a long time (a good 5–10 minutes), beat well after adding each egg, mix as minimally as possible after adding the flour, don't overbake and use soaked cake strips around the cake tins. This makes a big difference and is easy to do – just soak in water then wrap around the outside of the tin and bake.

DIFFICULTY 🐾 🐾

This cake isn't super difficult, and the Victoria Sponge is a simple classic. You just need to stack this taller, and remember that you're working with whipped cream, which isn't as stable as buttercream, so decisions about cat placement need to be made decisively.

SERVES: 18 (MAKES 3 X 23-CM [9-IN] CAKES)

Can be made gluten-free

VICTORIA SPONGE
400g [1¾ cups] unsalted butter,
  softened, at room temperature,
  plus extra for greasing
big pinch of salt
400g [2 cups] caster or granulated
  sugar
1 Tbsp vanilla bean paste
400g [14oz] eggs (from about
  7 medium eggs)

360g [2¾ cups] self-raising flour (to
  make gluten-free, substitute with a
  gluten-free self-raising flour blend
  plus ½ tsp xanthan gum)
40g [½ cup minus 2 tsp] cornflour
  [cornstarch] (or replace with
  self-raising flour; the cornflour helps
  to make the sponge extra light)
3 tsp baking powder (or gluten-free
  baking powder)
3–4 Tbsp whole milk

FILLING AND DECORATION
240g [¾ cup plus 4 tsp] good-quality
  strawberry jam
800ml [3½ cups] double [heavy]
  cream
icing [confectioners'] sugar,
  for dusting
handful each of strawberries,
  blueberries and raspberries

FONDANT LION AND CATS
see page 15

Continued overleaf

1 / Preheat the oven to 160°C [325°F/Gas mark 3]. Grease the base and sides of 3 x 23-cm [9-in] round cake tins with butter and line the bases with a circle of baking paper.

2 / Add the butter, salt and sugar to a large bowl and, using an electric whisk (or stand mixer fitted with a balloon whisk attachment), whisk until fluffy and pale in colour, scraping down the bowl a couple of times to ensure everything is whisked well. It's important not to under whisk at this stage, as you need to incorporate as much air as possible. Whisk in the vanilla.

3 / Add the eggs, one at a time, whisking well after each addition. The mixture may look slightly curdled after adding the last egg, but don't worry, this is normal.

4 / Sift in the flour (plus xanthan gum, if gluten-free), cornflour and baking powder, then using a spatula, fold in gently. Be careful to mix only until just combined.

5 / Add enough milk until the batter drops easily off the spatula when it's lifted up.

6 / Divide the batter evenly between the 3 prepared tins. Ideally, wrap the outside of each tin in a damp tea [dish] towel (or use cake strips – see intro) as this will ensure your cake bakes and rises evenly and taller, rather than doming in the middle. If you don't use cake strips, your cake domes will need trimming, so the overall cake will be a little flatter, but this is fine and will still be delicious!

7 / Bake for 20–25 minutes until the cakes visibly come away from the sides and a knife inserted into the centre comes out clean.

8 / Remove the cakes from the oven and leave to stand in their tins for 10 minutes, then carefully run a knife around the edges and turn them out onto wire racks. Peel off the baking paper and leave to cool completely.

9 / While the cakes are cooling, make the fondant cats and a lion following the instructions on page 15 (or take the chill option and use plastic toy versions instead!).

10 / Make sure the cakes are cool before assembling. Place one layer on a serving plate, then spoon over half the jam, spreading it to the edges. Whip the cream until soft peaks form, then spoon a small amount into a piping [pastry] bag. Cut a large tip (or use a large round piping tip), then pipe blobs of cream all around the circumference of the cake. Arrange cats/lion sticking out over the side of the cake. Pipe or spoon cream into the centre.

Tip: Fill your piping bag with small amounts of cream at a time – the squeezing action can cause the cream at the top of the bag to end up overwhipped if the bag is too full.

11 / Place the second layer of cake on top and repeat, using all the remaining jam, and arranging more cats. Place the third layer of cake on top, then dust the whole cake with icing sugar. Spoon the remaining cream into the centre and top with a pile of strawberries, blueberries and raspberries. Place a cat or 2 on top of the mountain of fruit. Best eaten the day it's made.

CAT TIP *If your cream does overwhip, just add more unwhipped cream and fold through with a spatula.*

- CAKES -

Tiger Stripes Cake

This cake is a real showstopper, *pawticularly* for fans of cats, tigers or unicorns. Not only is the outside of this cake striking, there's a second roar of excitement when you slice into it and reveal the tiger-striped pattern inside. Followed by the silence of happy people digging their forks into this mouthwatering orange, black sesame and chocolate cake.

DIFFICULTY 🐾 🐾 🐾 🐾

There's a bunch of steps and decorating, but ultimately you're just decorating one big tiger, so stay fierce to match its fierceness and hang in there. Chill the buttercream fully before you start adding the tiger face, and that'll help you out lots.

SERVES: AROUND 18 (MAKES 3 X 18-CM [7-IN] CAKES)

Can be made gluten-free

CAKE
300g [1⅓ cups] salted butter, cubed and softened, at room temperature, plus extra for greasing
300g [1½ cups] caster or granulated sugar
300g [10½oz] eggs (from about 4–5 medium eggs)
1 Tbsp vanilla bean paste
300g [2¼ cups] self-raising flour (to make gluten-free, substitute with a gluten-free self-raising flour blend plus ½ tsp xanthan gum)
120g [½ cup] whole plain yogurt

TO ADD TO THE ORANGE BATTER (ORANGE FLAVOURED)
finely grated zest of 1 orange
orange gel food dye

TO ADD TO THE BLACK BATTER (BLACK SESAME AND COCOA)
2 Tbsp unsweetened cocoa powder (ideally ultra Dutched black cocoa powder, as it's darker in colour, although any will do)
2 Tbsp hot water
3 Tbsp roasted black sesame paste (buy pre-roasted black sesame seeds, or toast them in a frying pan [skillet], then use a food processor to process into a paste)
black gel food dye

ITALIAN MERINGUE BUTTERCREAM
1 quantity, see page 24
black, orange and pink gel food dyes
unsweetened cocoa powder (optional)

UNICORN HORN
70g [½ cup] icing [confectioners'] sugar
2–4 tsp water
1 plain ice-cream cone (or use a gluten-free ice-cream cone)
sprinkles of your choice

1 / Preheat the oven to 160°C [325°F/Gas mark 3] and grease 3 x 18-cm [7-in] cake tins with butter. Line the bases with a circle of baking paper.

2 / Place the butter and sugar in a stand mixer fitted with a balloon whisk attachment (or use a handheld electric whisk) and beat until the butter is very fluffy and pale in colour.

Tip: It's crucial to beat this until it's as fluffy and light in colour as possible. To incorporate enough air, you should be beating for 5–10 minutes. Keep going until it's definitely not getting any fluffier or lighter.

3 / Add the eggs, one at a time, beating well after each addition. Add the vanilla and mix to combine.

4 / Sift in the flour (plus xanthan gum, if gluten-free) and gently fold in with a spatula. Stir through the yogurt until just combined.

5 / Divide the batter between 3 bowls, aiming to have roughly 50% less in one of the bowls. Set the bowl with the smaller amount aside as this one will stay white. In one of

Continued overleaf

the other bowls, stir through the orange zest and orange food dye. Separately, mix the cocoa powder and hot water together in a small bowl until smooth, then add it to the remaining bowl of batter. Add the black sesame paste and black food dye and stir through. You want to aim for vibrant orange and deep black – good-quality food dyes will help you out here!

6 / You should now have black, orange and white batters. Place 2 Tbsp of the black batter into the centre of each prepared cake tin. Place 2 Tbsp of the orange batter directly on top. Repeat with layering the black and orange batters, then add 2 Tbsp of white batter on top. Repeat this sequence until all the batter is used up. You can shake the tin a little from side to side to even out the batter, but there's no need to spread it out with a spoon.

7 / Bake the cakes for 30–40 minutes until golden and pulling away from the sides of the tin. Leave in the tins for 5 minutes, then carefully run a knife around the sides of the tins and turn out onto wire racks. Peel off the baking paper and leave to cool.

8 / Meanwhile, make the Italian meringue buttercream following the instructions on page 24.

9 / Place a 2 Tbsp of the buttercream in 2 separate bowls. Mix in black food dye to one bowl (you can add cocoa powder to deepen the base

colour as well), while keeping the other bowl white. Add orange food dye to the main/largest bowl of buttercream.

10 / Once the cakes are cool, use a serrated knife to level the tops. Stack the cakes with orange buttercream in between each layer, then coat the whole of the outside in a layer of orange buttercream, smoothing out first the sides then the top with a cake scraper. Don't worry about getting this first layer totally smooth, it's mostly there to lock in any crumbs.

11 / Place in the fridge until the buttercream is firm, then add another layer of orange buttercream and smooth the top in the same way again, followed by the sides. To get an extra smooth finish, warm a metal cake smoother or scraper under hot water and use this to smooth over again. After smoothing the sides, you will be left with a rough edge of buttercream around the top – leave this without smoothing it in. Place in the fridge to firm up.

12 / Meanwhile, for the unicorn horn, make an icing by mixing the icing sugar and a little water together in a bowl until smooth. It should be thinner than a piping icing, but not so thin that it drips everywhere! Cover the surface of the ice-cream cone with the icing, then roll in the sprinkles or scatter with sprinkles to cover it completely and leave to set.

13 / Once the cake is chilled (the buttercream should be

firm to the touch), you're ready to pipe on all the details in buttercream. Use a cocktail stick [toothpick] to mark out where you will place the different facial features, then use a palette knife to spread on the white buttercream for the mouth area.

14 / Put the black buttercream into a piping [pastry] bag and cut a small tip. Pipe on the eyes, nose and black markings/details. Put some leftover orange buttercream into another piping bag and cut a large tip. Use this to pipe the ears, pulling upwards and squeezing less to create the tapered look. Pipe round ball shapes for the paws. If the ears or paws need a little extra shaping, use a palette knife to help you. Drag the tip of a narrow palette knife to create the indentations in the paws. Add pink food dye to a small amount of the white buttercream and put this in a piping bag. Cut a small tip and pipe the tongue. Put a little leftover white buttercream in a piping bag, cut a small tip and use to add additional details.

15 / To complete the look, pop the unicorn horn you made earlier on top! Store in an airtight container for up to 5 days.

TIGER TIP *"If the layer of buttercream is chilled enough, you can carefully scrape off any mistakes you made with my face and start again!"*

"Make me and you've earned your stripes as a baker."

Eye of the Tiger Roll

This cake roll is made using a chiffon cake technique, along with a special technique to swirl the colours, so it's very different to a standard Swiss [jelly] roll. It's soft as a pillow, not to mention stripy and striking. It's typical that two mini tigers would settle down on top of it, really.

To make sure the pattern comes out nicely and the cake rolls without a big crack, be sure to read and reread the recipe first before you start! But if it does crack, don't worry – your new-found tiger buddies will help conceal it.

DIFFICULTY 🐾 🐾 🐾 🐾
This is higher due to the beating and folding in of the egg whites, swirling the batter, rolling the sponge and piping the buttercream tigers. But as long as you read the instructions carefully and make sure you have everything prepared, you should be able to channel your inner tiger. To make this easier, you can substitute the tigers for any of the easier cat recipes (see Cat Basics, starting on page 8) or use plastic figurines.

SERVES: 8–10

Can be made gluten-free

CAKE: FOR THE COLOUR
1 Tbsp unsweetened cocoa powder (ideally ultra Dutched black cocoa powder, as it's darker in colour, although any will do)
2 Tbsp hot water
black and orange food dyes

CAKE: EGG YOLK MIXTURE
butter, for greasing
5 medium egg yolks
35g [2½ Tbsp] caster or granulated sugar
pinch of salt

60ml [¼ cup] vegetable oil
60ml [¼ cup] whole milk
2 tsp orange blossom water
100g [¾ cup] plain [all-purpose] flour (to make gluten-free, substitute with a gluten-free plain flour blend plus ¼ tsp xanthan gum)
2 tsp cornflour [cornstarch]

CAKE: EGG WHITE MIXTURE
5 medium egg whites
65g [⅓ cup plus 1 tsp] caster or granulated sugar

FILLING
6 Tbsp fine-cut marmalade (or your favourite choice of jam)
300ml [1¼ cups] double [heavy] cream
30g [3½ Tbsp] icing [confectioners'] sugar
1 Tbsp vanilla bean paste

PLUS
Buttercream, Fondant/Marzipan, Meowringue or 3D Cookie Cats (see pages 12–25)
sprinkles of choice (optional)

CAT FACT: Tigers have white spots of fur on the back of each ear that look like fake eyes. These are called 'ocelli' and are there to scare off other animals.

Continued overleaf

1 / Preheat the oven to 160°C [325°F/Gas mark 3]. Grease the base and sides of a 27 x 35-cm [10¾ x 14-in] Swiss roll tin [jelly roll pan] with butter and line with baking paper, covering the base and extending beyond the 2 longer sides.

2 / First, for the cake colour, stir the cocoa powder and hot but not boiling water together in a bowl. Set aside.

3 / Add all the 'cake: egg yolk mixture' ingredients to a large bowl and whisk until smooth.

4 / In a separate bowl, make the 'cake: egg white mixture'. Use a handheld electric whisk or stand mixer fitted with the balloon whisk attachment to whisk the egg whites on medium speed until foamy. Add the caster sugar and continue whisking until soft peaks form. For this cake, you want the peaks to flop over slightly at the tips, rather than point straight upwards. If you whisk beyond this point, you may get cracks in your finished cake when rolling.

5 / Fold the egg whites into the egg yolk mixture, a third at a time. Your finished batter should be of pourable consistency, but still fluffy and full of air from the egg whites. Pour 200g [7oz] into a separate bowl and stir in the cocoa powder mixture until combined. Add enough black food dye to colour it a deep black colour. Stir the orange food dye through the mixture in the first bowl. Be careful to fold gently and not any more than is necessary.

6 / Pour the orange batter into the prepared tin and spread out evenly. Pour the black batter on top and spread out to cover the orange batter completely (don't worry too much about the edges as they will be sliced off later!). Spread it out gently with the back of a spoon, trying not to disturb the batter underneath. Use a chopstick or the handle of a spoon to swirl the batter: drag the chopstick or spoon left and right along the longest side, working your way from top to bottom, then repeat the same motion along the shortest side. Bang the tin against your work surface once to release any large air bubbles.

7 / Bake immediately for 20 minutes, or until the cake in the middle of the tin is spongy and springs back. Using the sides of the baking paper, lift the cake onto a wire rack and leave to cool.

8 / When the cake is cool, place a sheet of baking paper on top, then a chopping [cutting] board (or any flat board) and flip the whole cake over. Peel off the layer of baking paper that the cake was baked on, then trim all the edges (they are drier, so leaving them could cause the cake to crack). On one of the shorter ends, cut 5 shallow slits into the cake, then spread over the marmalade. Add the cream, icing sugar and vanilla to a bowl and whip to soft peaks. Spread two-thirds of the cream on top of the marmalade, adding a thicker amount of cream on the side

with the slits. Roll the cake up from one of the shorter sides using the baking paper to help you. Don't roll the cake too tightly, otherwise it will crack.

9 / Place the roll on a serving tray and trim the ends off so that the spiral shows clearly. Decoratively pipe the remaining cream on top and nestle in your chosen tigers/cats). If making buttercream tigers, follow the general steps on page 23, just changing the markings to make these look like tigers. It's best to pipe these on a square of baking paper, chill in the freezer for 15 minutes until solid, then easily transfer to the cake. Add sprinkles to finish, if you like. Best eaten straight away, or cover and store in the fridge and eat the following day.

Ghost Cat Pumpkin Cupcakes

Don't be trick or treated into thinking that just because these are cute that they aren't also full of pumpkin cake deliciousness that'll lift your spirits. And you'll be happy to hear that for the cake batter, you simply put all the dry ingredients into one bowl, all the wet in the other and mix together. Easy!

If you're a fan of cats (and adorable ghost cats), pumpkins and Halloween, then these are for you!

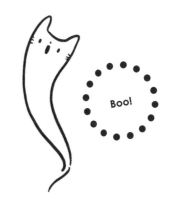

Boo!

DIFFICULTY 🐾 🐾, **if using fondant, or** 🐾 🐾 🐾 🐾
The harder rating is down to the *Meowringue Ghost Cats* (page 16). Rest assured, the cake batter is extremely easy to make, and you're just piping a swirly whirl of buttercream on top. To make them easier (🐾 🐾), make fondant ghost cats instead (page 15).

MAKES: 20–24 LARGE CUPCAKES/MUFFINS

Can be made vegan and/or gluten-free

CAKE: WET INGREDIENTS
200g [7oz] canned unsweetened pumpkin purée
180ml [¾ cup] sunflower oil (or other neutral-tasting oil)
1¾ tsp white wine vinegar
260ml [1 cup plus 1 Tbsp] milk (or any plant-based milk)
1 Tbsp vanilla bean paste
¼ tsp salt

CAKE: DRY INGREDIENTS
300g [2¼ cups] self-raising flour (to make gluten-free, substitute with a gluten-free self-raising flour blend plus ½ tsp xanthan gum)
340g [1¾ cups minus ½ Tbsp] light brown sugar
1¼ Tbsp baking powder
2 tsp ground cinnamon
¼ tsp ground nutmeg
¼ tsp ground ginger
pinch of ground cloves
200g [7oz] dark [bittersweet or semisweet] chocolate, roughly chopped (optional)

CREAM CHEESE FROSTING
180g [¾ cup plus 2 tsp] butter (or vegan butter – use one that's close to 80% fat content)
450g [3¼ cups] icing [confectioners'] sugar
340g [1½ cups] whole cream cheese (or use whole vegan cream cheese)
1 tsp vanilla bean paste
orange food dye

TO DECORATE
sprinkles of choice
Meowringue Ghost Cats (page 16), or make from fondant (page 15)

Continued overleaf

- CAKES -

1 / Preheat the oven to 170°C [340°F/Gas mark 3], then line 2 x 12-hole muffin tins with paper cases.

2 / Add all the wet ingredients and the salt to a large bowl, then whisk together.

3 / In a separate large bowl, stir together all the dry ingredients.

4 / Add the dry ingredients to the wet and whisk until just combined. Divide the batter straight away among the cupcake cases, to about three-quarters full. You should have around 20–24 in total, depending on the size of your paper cases/tins. Bake for

25–30 minutes until risen and a knife inserted into the centre of a cupcake comes out clean. Transfer to wire racks and leave to cool completely.

5 / Meanwhile, make the cream cheese frosting. Beat the butter and icing sugar together in a stand mixer fitted with a balloon whisk attachment (or use a handheld electric whisk) until very light and fluffy. Add the cream cheese and vanilla and whisk until fluffy again. Don't overwhisk after adding the cream cheese, otherwise it can go grainy and flat. Whisk in orange food dye to colour.

6 / Place the buttercream in a large piping [pastry] bag with large piping tip (a 1M or 2D piping tip works well) and pipe a tall swirl on top of each cupcake, starting from the outside, then circling inwards and upwards.

7 / Decorate with sprinkles of your choice and ghost cat meringues. Store in an airtight container in the fridge for up to 3 days.

Note: Feel free to tweak and accessorize the decoration however you like!

Cat Beach Paradise Cake

Everyone who loves cats has dreamed of going to a beach or island inhabited by cats. You may or may not get to visit an island like this in your lifetime, but you're only ever a whisker away from creating it in delicious moist chocolate cake and jelly form. This cake may look complex, but it's actually high impact and not difficult to make. It's a simple chunk of cake carved out, then scruffily covered in ganache and cookie crumbs. The jelly pouring takes a little preparation, but even if a little leaks out, it still works out fine in the end. Just follow the steps and trust the process to reach Cat Paradise.

For this cake, you'll need food-grade acetate on a roll!

DIFFICULTY 🐾 🐾 🐾 🐾

SERVES: 14–16 (MAKES 2 X 23-CM [9-IN] CAKES, PLUS CAKE OFFCUTS TO ENJOY!)

Can be made gluten-free

CHOCOLATE CAKE
1 quantity of the Kitty-Kat cake
(page 58), baked in 2 x 23-cm
[9-in] cake tins and cooled

WHITE CHOCOLATE GANACHE
500g [1lb 2oz] white chocolate, very
finely chopped
160ml [¾ cup minus 1 Tbsp] double
[heavy] cream (or coconut milk)

JELLY
1.2 litres [5 cups] water
200g [1 cup] caster or granulated
sugar
3 tsp agar agar powder
large pieces of peel of 1 orange
and 1 lemon
turquoise, blue and green gel
food dyes

CATS
Cookie, Fondant, or Meowringue
Cats (pages 12, 15 or 16)
you could also make
Marshmeowllow Cats (page 19)
but these would be a bit bigger
in size as they are hard to
make smaller

PLUS
100g [3½oz] any pale or sand-
coloured cookies (e.g. digestives
[graham crackers], shortbread,
gluten-free cookies), to crush
sweets [candies], to decorate with
(you can get creative and use
different sweets and cookies that
you have in your cupboard, but
I used peach rings, pink wafers,
rainbow belts and Swedish fish)
cocktail stick umbrellas (optional)

> **CAT TIP** You can use some of the leftover white chocolate ganache to shape a sandcastle, then cover it with the 'sand' crumbs.

Continued overleaf

- CAKES -

1 / Make and bake the cakes following the instructions on pages 58–60. Make the cats following the instructions on pages 12, 15 or 16, ready to decorate with later.

2 / Crush the cookies in a food processor or place in a bag and bash with a rolling pin.

3 / Next, for the ganache, place the chocolate in a large heatproof bowl. Heat the cream (or coconut milk) in a pan on the stove, until JUST starting to bubble around the edges, then immediately pour onto the chocolate. Leave for 2 minutes, then stir until all the chocolate has melted. If the chocolate isn't very finely chopped, there will likely still be pieces of unmelted chocolate. If this happens, place in the microwave for 3-second bursts, stirring well after each (or stir over a very low heat on the stove). Be careful because chocolate, and especially white chocolate, can easily get too hot and end up splitting!

4 / Once the ganache is smooth, leave to cool at room temperature until it's a nice spreadable consistency – it still needs to be slightly runny so that the cake doesn't tear as you spread the ganache, but not so runny that it just drips off. (This white chocolate ganache has a very low amount of cream to chocolate as we want it to set very firm!) If the ganache becomes too firm, give it a couple 3-second blasts in the microwave.

5 / Take your cooled cakes. Use a serrated knife to cut the top off one cake, so it is flat. Place on a serving tray and spread a layer of ganache on top. Place the second cake layer on top, then carve the cake where you want the sea to be. You want the cut-out to reach the centre of the cake, and carve it as low as possible while still leaving a bit of cake at the bottom so that it remains round.

6 / Cover the exposed cake with ganache (you can be messy here; it doesn't need to be smooth). Cut a piece of clear food-grade acetate to a little longer than the total circumference of the cake and wrap this around the entire cake, pressing to ensure it sticks to the ganache all the way around. Use a clip or tape to hold the overlapping ends of the acetate together. If there are any gaps between the acetate and the ganache where jelly could escape, make sure to fill these with a little more ganache. For extra jelly-proofing security, if you used a cake tin with a removable base, then place the outer circle around the acetate to help hold it in place (or you can use an adjustable entremet ring, but this isn't essential). Chill in the fridge until very firm or chill in the freezer for 15 minutes.

7 / For the jelly, add the water, sugar and agar agar powder to a pan and stir to disperse the powder. Add the citrus peels and stir occasionally over a high heat until the sugar and agar agar have dissolved,

then bring to a boil. Boil for 30 seconds, then remove from the heat and take out the citrus peels.

8 / Divide the mixture between three shallow bowls (the more shallow the mixture, the quicker it will set), while leaving a quarter of the mixture in the warm pan. The jelly mixture should be divided equally between the three bowls and the pan. Leave the pan on the stove over the lowest heat. Add green, blue and turquoise food dyes to the different bowls: you want one bowl to be dark for the bottom of the sea, a medium tone for the middle layer, then a light blue for the top layer.

9 / Leave the jellies to set in the bowls at room temperature. They will start to set just below 40°C [104°F], but you can pop them into the fridge to set faster, if you like. Meanwhile, sprinkle cookie sand crumbs onto the raised flat area of the cake where the beach will be. Once the jellies are set firm, use a knife to cut into rough cube shapes, then pour them onto the cake where the sea will be, starting with the darkest blue and ending with the lightest. The jelly cubes should reach just below where the beach starts.

10 / Place fish-shaped sweets or jellies on the top most layer and/or next to the front edge of the acetate, so they will be visible. Place the cake back in the fridge or freezer while you bring the pouring jelly to temperature.

Continued overleaf

11 / Pour a quarter of the clear jelly from the pan into a bowl to start bringing the temperature down. Once it's at 40°C [104°F] (or slightly tepid to touch), pour it over the jelly cubes (use a funnel to help you). Chill in the fridge to speed up the setting. A small amount of jelly may leak out, but don't worry about this as it will form a nice seal for the next layer, so the jelly doesn't just leak out at the end. Once this layer is completely set, pour over more jelly until it reaches almost beach level (you will likely have more than enough jelly, just in case). Chill in the fridge again until set firm.

12 / Simply peel off the acetate and reveal! Add more cookie crumbs to cover the sharp edge between the sea and beach, then place cats chilling on beach towels or floating in rubber rings in the sea. Make fun beach accessories and huts and give your cat beach paradise a name!

13 / This is best eaten the same day the jelly is poured in – but you can prep the rest of the cake the day before and store in the fridge, then add the jelly and final decorations to serve.

CAT TIP *"After unmoulding, agar agar jelly often seeps out a little bit of liquid. Don't worry about this – this is normal and our beach won't suddenly melt! The drips at the bottom will look like seaweed on the ocean floor. You can also make this cake with a firm gelatine-based jelly, but agar agar is ideal for parties as more people can eat it!"*

- CAKES -

Happy *Purrthday* Cake

Want to quickly rustle up a decadently moist and beautifully spiced birthday cake for the cat-loving person in your life (or for yourself)? This cake is full of warming ginger, sweet and salty caramel, and addictive biscoff – a combination that both kids and adults won't be able to resist. Did I also mention that this cake can easily be made vegan? No one would be able to tell the difference…

The decoration on top is like painting a simple oil painting but in buttercream that you can eat – and remember that asymmetrical faces are all part of the charm, so there's no need to be too exact.

DIFFICULTY ❀ ❀ ❀
This cake itself is mainly a one-bowl mixture – the only challenge is decorating it! The sprinkles help cover any rough edges at the bottom of the cake.

SERVES: 10–12 (MAKES 2 X 18-CM [7-IN] CAKES)

Can be made vegan and/or gluten-free

SPICED GINGER CAKE
softened butter, for greasing
360ml [1½ cups] milk (or plant-based milk)
2 tsp white wine vinegar
40g [2 Tbsp] black treacle [molasses]
150ml [⅔ cup minus 2 tsp] sunflower oil (or other neutral-tasting oil)
½ tsp salt
½ Tbsp vanilla bean paste
330g [2½ cups] self-raising flour (to make gluten-free, substitute with a gluten-free self-raising flour blend that contains added xanthan gum, plus ½ tsp xanthan gum)

55g [¼ cup plus 1 tsp] caster or granulated sugar
250g [1¼ cups] soft dark brown sugar (or muscovado)
1 Tbsp baking powder (or use gluten-free baking powder)
2½ Tbsp ground ginger
¾ Tbsp ground cinnamon

CARAMEL
25ml [2⅔ Tbsp] water
80g [⅔ cup] caster or granulated sugar
40g [¼ cup] coconut cream (use just the thick part on top)
10g [1 Tbsp] butter
pinch of salt, to taste

BUTTERCREAM
250g [1 cup plus 2 Tbsp] butter, at room temperature, cubed (or vegan butter – use one that's close to 80% fat content)
500g [3½ cups] icing [confectioners'] sugar
a little milk or plant-based milk
1 Tbsp vanilla bean paste
100g [3½oz] biscoff spread (this is added to a third of the buttercream; omit this if making the recipe gluten-free)

PLUS
your choice of sprinkles and gel food dyes

1 / Preheat the oven to 170°C [340°F/Gas mark 3]. Grease the bases and sides of 2 x 18-cm [7-in] cake tins with butter and line the bases with a circle of baking paper.

2 / Add the milk and white wine vinegar to a large bowl and whisk together. Add the treacle, oil, salt and vanilla, then whisk again until combined.

3 / In a separate large bowl, combine the self-raising flour (plus xanthan gum, if gluten-free), caster sugar, dark brown sugar, baking powder, ginger and cinnamon. Add the wet ingredients to the dry

Continued overleaf

ingredients and whisk until just combined. Divide straight away between the 2 prepared tins and bake for 30–35 minutes (don't open the oven in the middle of baking as it may sink) until springy on top and a knife inserted into the centre comes out clean. Leave the cakes in their tins for 5 minutes, then carefully run a knife around the edges and turn out onto wire racks. Peel off the baking paper and leave to cool completely.

4 / Meanwhile, make the caramel. Add the water and caster sugar to a saucepan and swirl the pan just to make sure all the sugar is hydrated with the water. Once the mixture starts to bubble (do not stir at all, otherwise the sugar will crystallize), increase the heat and wait until the sugar turns an amber colour. You can swill the pan around to even out the colour towards the end. Add the coconut cream to a small separate bowl. When the sugar syrup has turned a deep amber colour, remove the pan from the heat and add all the coconut cream in one go. Stir constantly with a balloon whisk. The sauce will bubble up so be careful at this stage! Continue stirring until it is a smooth and creamy sauce. Add the butter and stir until dissolved. Pour the sauce into a medium bowl and sprinkle with a little salt to taste. Cover with plastic wrap and chill in the fridge for around 30 minutes. It will thicken as it cools.

5 / Next, make the buttercream. Add the butter and icing sugar to a large bowl and beat with a handheld electric whisk until pale and fluffy (or use a stand mixer fitted with a balloon whisk attachment). Add a little milk to make the consistency easier to spread. Transfer 150g of buttercream to a separate bowl and whisk in the biscoff spread. The biscoff can stiffen the buttercream, so you can add an additional 2 tsp of milk to make it easier to spread. Then add the vanilla to the remaning (larger amount of) buttercream, plus a little milk again to help with the consistency.

6 / Once the cakes are completely cool, level the tops with a serrated knife. To assemble, place the first cake layer on a flat serving board, spread the biscoff buttercream on top (making it thicker at the sides than the centre), drizzle the caramel in the centre and place the second cake layer on top. Spread the vanilla buttercream in a thin layer over the top and sides to 'crumb coat'. As this is the first coat, it doesn't need to be extremely neat, and you will see crumbs coming through.

7 / Chill the cake in the fridge for at least 1 hour, or in the freezer for 10 minutes until the buttercream is chilled and firm. Then cover the whole cake in another layer of vanilla buttercream to cover most of

the crumbs. Use a palette knife (heating it under hot water for a smoother finish) to smooth the buttercream around the sides, then smooth the buttercream on the top, smoothing it in from the edges and towards the centre. (Make sure there is a little vanilla buttercream left for the decorations). Scatter sprinkles all along the bottom of the cake, then chill in the fridge for at least 1 hour again, or in the freezer for 10 minutes until the buttercream is firm.

8 / Meanwhile, divide the remaining vanilla buttercream between different bowls and add food dye to colour as desired. You will need one colour for the piped swirls and your colours for the cat design (black for the face features, and one colour to contrast).

9 / When the cake is chilled, use a cocktail stick [toothpick] to mark out your cat outline. Use a palette knife to spread buttercream within the outlines for the cat face. Chill the cake again in the fridge or freezer, then pipe the facial details on top. Place the black buttercream in a piping bag and cut a small tip then pipe the facial features to finish. You can customize this however you like; pipe extras, like a decorative border or a party hat, and sprinkles work a treat! Store in an airtight container in the fridge for up to a week, or three days at room temperature.

"I'll fur-give you if you make me look less cute than I am, but you can scrape errors off and keep going!"

The Korat Cake

I feel like every breed of cat must have a spiritual cake form. As Korat sounds closest to 'carrot', its spiritual form has got to be the most warming, luxurious and moist carrot cake. It's packed full of carrot and a harmonious blend of spices, then sandwiched and encased in a sweet but tangy cream cheese frosting. And the buttercream cats, carrots (and cats pretending to be carrots...) make it so that this cake's looks match up to its delicious interior. You will not be disappointed!

DIFFICULTY 🐾 🐾 🐾 🐾 🐾

This high rating is purely down to the decorating! If you're not feeling too confident piping buttercream cats (page 23) then try making a few less and have fun with it – after all they're cats, and cats look all sort of weird when they're sitting in their awkward ways! Any 'mistakes' are intentional. Embrace the *cat*-titude. OR decorate simply with plastic toy cats, sprinkles and candles! Do what you can to make a fun cake to make people smile.

SERVES: AROUND 12 (MAKES 2 X 23-CM [9-IN] CAKES)

Can be made gluten-free

CAKE

softened butter, for greasing
300g [2¼ cups] plain [all-purpose] flour (to make gluten-free, substitute with a gluten-free plain flour blend plus ½ tsp xanthan gum)
2 tsp baking powder (or use gluten-free baking powder)
1 tsp bicarbonate of soda [baking soda]
2½ tsp ground cinnamon
¼ tsp ground ginger
pinch of nutmeg
¼ tsp fine salt
100g [½ cup] caster or granulated sugar
300g [1½ cups] soft light brown sugar

300ml [1¼ cups] neutral-tasting vegetable oil
1 tsp vanilla bean paste
4 medium eggs
300g [2¼ cups] finely grated carrots (around 3–4 carrots, depending on size)
80g [¾ cup] pecans, roughly chopped (can be omitted if you prefer without)
70g [½ cup] raisins (can be omitted if you prefer without)

CREAM CHEESE FROSTING

250g [1 cup plus 2 Tbsp] butter, room temperature
590g [4¼ cups] icing [confectioners'] sugar
330g [1½ cups] whole cream cheese
1 tsp vanilla bean paste
green food dye

BUTTERCREAM CATS AND CARROTS

½ quantity of any buttercream from pages 24–25 – you will have some left over but you can keep this in the fridge for another bake!

PLUS

100g [1 cup plus 1 tsp] pecans, roughly chopped and toasted

CAT TIP *"Make sure the cake and cream cheese fur-osting is kept chilled... or I will melt and slip off."*

Continued overleaf

1 / Preheat the oven to 170°C [340°F/Gas mark 3]. Grease the base and sides of 2 x 23-cm [9-in] cake tins with butter and line the bases with a circle of baking paper.

2 / Mix the flour (plus xanthan gum, if gluten-free), baking powder, bicarbonate of soda, spices and salt together in a large bowl until combined.

3 / In a separate large bowl, whisk together the caster sugar, light brown sugar, oil and vanilla together, until combined. Add the eggs, one at a time, beating well after each addition.

4 / Sift in a third of the dry mixture into the wet and whisk to combine. Add the remaining dry mixture in 2 more batches, mixing just enough so that there is no visible flour. Avoid overmixing!

5 / Add the grated carrots, pecans (if using) and raisins (if using) and mix in one last time.

6 / Divide the batter between the 2 prepared cake tins and bake for 35–40 minutes until a skewer inserted into the centre comes out clean. Leave the cakes to cool in the tins for 10 minutes, then run a knife around the edges and turn out onto wire racks. Peel off the baking paper and leave to cool completely.

7 / Meanwhile, make the cream cheese frosting. Using a stand mixer fitted with a balloon whisk attachment (or a handheld electric whisk), beat the butter and icing sugar

together for around 10 minutes, or until very light in colour and fluffy. Add the cream cheese and vanilla and whisk until fluffy again. Don't overwhisk as it can go grainy and flat.

8 / Place one cake layer on a serving plate, then top with cream cheese frosting and sandwich with the second cake. Add green food dye to the remaining frosting and spread a thin layer all over the top and sides. Use a palette knife to smooth it all over. There will be crumbs and cake showing through the frosting – that's normal. Place in the fridge for 1 hour, or in the freezer for 15 minutes, or until the frosting feels firm.

9 / Cover the whole cake in another layer of frosting, starting by smoothing the top with the palette knife, then smoothing the sides. Heat the palette knife under hot water and pass over the cake again to help you get a smoother finish. Press the roughly chopped and toasted pecans into the sides around the base, then return to the fridge or freezer to chill again.

10 / Follow the instructions on page 23 for piping the cats. You can choose either of the buttercream recipes on pages 24–25, but the reason you will want to use buttercream over cream cheese frosting is that this will have more stability and structure, so you will find piping the cats a lot easier. Store the finished cake in an airtight container in the fridge for up to a week.

PIPING TIPS AND IDEAS:

1 / For the carrots, colour some of the buttercream orange, then put this into a piping [pastry] bag, cut a medium tip and pipe while pulling gradually upwards. To make the green stalks, colour a small amount of buttercream green and put this into a piping bag, this time with a grass tip attachment. Use this to pipe the stalks onto the body of the carrot. You can also pipe the stalks individually by just cutting a small tip on the piping bag. Create the indents on the carrots by pressing lightly with a butter knife.

2 / To make the cats, follow the instructions and tips on page 23. Just pipe the cats on a piece of baking paper, then place in the freezer for 15 minutes, or until completely chilled. Peel off the baking paper and place on the cake wherever you like. If you want a cat hanging off the side of the cake, you will need to pipe it directly onto the cake where you would like it. You can be totally creative with this, so have some of the cats holding carrots or pecans, pretending to be carrots, and chasing carrots. You can even carve into the cake and have cats digging out carrots from the ground, or make a little vegetable patch, and cats with carrot hats and necklaces. There are many ways to make this cake fun and unique. Start decorating and see where it takes you...

Purrito Swiss Roll

If giant cake rolls existed, it would surely be a favourite place for a cat to snuggle up. If you make sure to roll this Swiss [jelly] roll while it is still warm, it will 'remember' its shape so that it won't crack once rolled with the filling. Use a damp tea [dish] towel as this will keep the sponge moist – it is very light and has no fat so is prone to drying out! Don't forget to trim all the edges of the Swiss roll first, as these will be a little firmer than the rest of the cake, and may cause it to crack.

DIFFICULTY ❀ ❀ ❀

Can be made gluten-free

DECORATIVE PASTE
(optional if you want a patterned roll, but you can also skip this)
25g [2 Tbsp] butter, softened, plus extra for greasing
25g [2¾ Tbsp] icing [confectioners'] sugar
1 medium egg white
25g [3 Tbsp] plain [all-purpose] flour (to make gluten-free, substitute with a gluten-free plain flour blend – don't add xanthan gum)
pink gel food dye

SERVES: 8

CAKE
4 medium eggs
125g [⅔ cup minus 2 tsp] caster or granulated sugar
125g [1 cup minus 1 Tbsp] self-raising flour (to make gluten-free, substitute with a gluten-free self-raising flour blend – don't add xanthan gum)

FILLING
8 Tbsp raspberry jam
300ml [1¼ cups] double [heavy] cream
1 tsp vanilla bean paste
1 Marzipan or Fondant Cat (see page 15)

"If you do end up with a crack, no one will notice because I'm so adorable"

Continued overleaf

- CAKES -

51

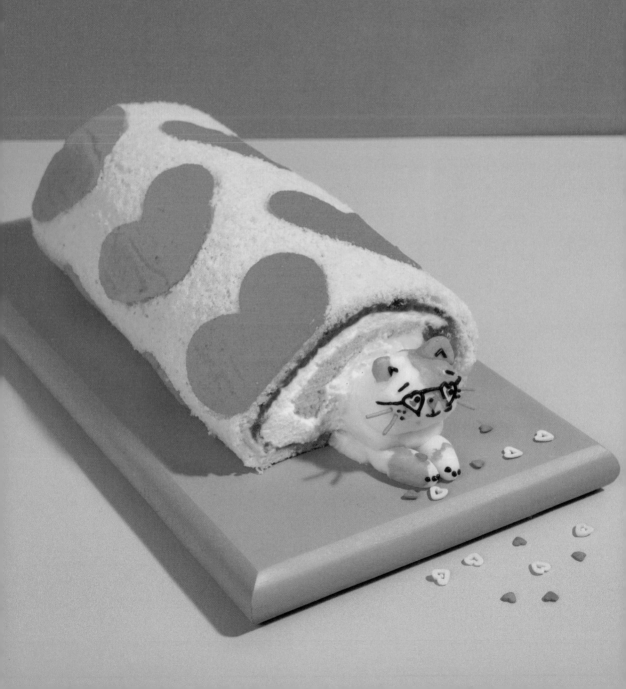

1 / Grease a rectangular 38 x 25-cm [15 x 10-in] Swiss roll tin [jelly roll pan] with butter, then line the base with baking paper. You can draw your design template on the back of the baking paper before placing it in the tin, unless you want to work freehand. Concentrate the design on just one half of the paper (landscape), as this is the side that will be visible once rolled.

2 / Make the decorative paste for the hearts (skip this if you're making a plain roll, the *purrito* cat remains the star after all!). Cream together the butter and icing sugar in a large bowl with a wooden spoon or flexible spatula until light and fluffy. Mix in the egg white, then add the flour and whisk until just combined. Add food dye to colour the paste as desired, then transfer the mixture to a piping [pastry] bag. Cut a tip and pipe your design. I've gone for simple hearts, but you can pipe anything you like. Chill in the fridge or freezer until firm, while you make the cake.

3 / Preheat the oven to 180°C [350°F/Gas mark 4].

4 / For the cake, using a handheld electric whisk or stand mixer fitted with a whisk attachment, whisk the eggs and sugar together in a large bowl on high speed for about 7 minutes, or until very thick and light in colour and holds a trail. Sift in the self-raising flour, then carefully fold it in to avoid deflating the batter too much.

5 / Spread the batter over the top of the frozen piped design. Bang the tray a couple of times on the work surface to pop any large air bubbles, and bake for 10–12 minutes until evenly golden, spongy on top and coming away from the edges.

6 / Once baked, carefully turn the cake out onto a chopping [cutting] board lined with baking paper, and remove the baking paper to reveal your design. Place a clean damp tea [dish] towel on top of a second board, hold this on top of the sponge and quickly flip the board over. The sponge is now upside down and the design is resting on the damp tea towel. Trim all the cake edges, then immediately roll up in the tea towel (starting from the side without the decoration). Leave the cake to completely cool while wrapped in the tea towel.

7 / When the cake is cool, carefully unroll it and spread with the jam. Whip the double cream and vanilla together until soft peaks form, then spread the cream over the top of the jam – make it slightly thicker at the end which you will start rolling the cake up from (the end that doesn't have the pattern on the back). Make sure not to make the initial roll very tight, so you can fit your cat into it later.

8 / Make a fondant or marzipan cat following the instructions on page 15. You will just need the head, part of the body and the front paws (it will look weird until it's in the cake!). Insert your cat into one end of the Swiss roll so that the head and paws are visible. You can make any kind of fondant cat you like: happy, sleepy, angry, angelic or cool with sunglasses. Best eaten the day it's made.

The Raga-Muffin

Ragamuffins are a breed of cat, whose sweet nature must surely be represented by the fluffiest, most comforting, bakery-style muffin. The secret of these is the combination of both butter and oil, which locks in moisture, and the acidity from the lemon juice/white wine vinegar, which reacts with the baking powder to give extra fluffiness and rise. This base recipe is also extremely versatile (just like ragamuffin cats). You can add in any fresh or frozen berries that you have to hand, and switch up the flavours. Possibly best of all? This recipes requires just two bowls, so there's minimal washing-up and no stand mixer needed.

Like all the recipes in this book, you can vary the decoration on these cupcakes, using your favourite colours for the ragamuffin cat, and try out different sprinkles for different effects and facial expressions.

DIFFICULTY 🐾 🐾

MAKES: AROUND 16 MUFFINS (MAY VARY SLIGHTLY DEPENDING ON SIZE OF MUFFIN CASES AND IF ANY BERRIES ARE ADDED)

Can be made gluten-free

MUFFINS
250ml [1 cup plus 2 tsp] whole milk
1½ Tbsp lemon juice or white wine vinegar
50ml [3½ Tbsp] vegetable oil (or any neutral-tasting oil)
60g [¼ cup] butter, melted
½ tsp salt
1 tsp vanilla bean paste
3 medium eggs
300g [2¼ cups] plain [all-purpose] flour (to make gluten-free, substitute with a gluten-free plain flour blend plus ½ tsp xanthan gum)

3 tsp baking powder (or gluten-free baking powder)
160g [1 cup plus 2 Tbsp] caster or granulated sugar

BUTTERCREAM
½ quantity of your choice of buttercream (see pages 24–25)
pink and black gel food dyes

PLUS
black sugar strand sprinkles, for whiskers (or you can pipe them in black buttercream, or find something similar)
edible eye sprinkles (optional)
your choice of additional sprinkles (optional)

CAT TIP For different flavours, try adding 5 Tbsp of any freeze-dried fruit pieces or powder, the grated zest of a lemon or orange, and/or fresh or frozen berries – just coat a few berries in flour and push into the top of the cupcake just before baking.

Continued overleaf

1 / Preheat the oven to 200°C [400°F/Gas mark 6] (unless you are chilling your batter – see step 5 – in which case preheat the oven later). Line muffin tins with 16 paper cases (if you have large tins then this recipe will make fewer muffins, and if your tins are smaller, the recipe will make more).

2 / Pour the milk into a large bowl, then add the lemon juice or vinegar on top and mix. Add the oil, melted butter, salt and vanilla, then add the eggs and whisk with a balloon whisk until combined.

3 / In a separate bowl, whisk the flour (plus xanthan gum, if gluten-free), baking powder and caster sugar together.

4 / Add the dry ingredients to the wet and whisk until just combined.

5 / For extra fluffy and tall muffins, chill the batter in the freezer for 20–30 minutes, or in the fridge for at least 1 hour, but if you're in a rush you can skip this step and they will still turn out incredible.

6 / Fill each muffin case with the batter until they are three-quarters full. Bake for around 20 minutes, or until risen, golden and firm on top and a skewer inserted into the centre doesn't have any wet batter clinging to it.

7 / When baked, transfer the muffins to a wire rack and leave to cool completely.

8 / Meanwhile, make the buttercream following the instructions on pages 24–25.

9 / Place around 1 Tbsp of buttercream in a small bowl and colour it pink, then place 1 Tbsp of the buttercream in another bowl and colour black. Put both into separate piping [pastry] bags fitted with small round piping tips, or just cut the end so there's a small opening to pipe details.

10 / Spoon 2 Tbsp of the white buttercream into a piping bag fitted with a medium piping tip, or cut the tip to a medium size (this is for piping the ears and nose and mouth area). Put the remaining white buttercream into another piping bag fitted with a grass piping tip.

11 / Using the largest piping bag fitted with the grass piping tip, pipe strands of white buttercream to look like fur, starting from the centre of the muffins and working outwards. Use the smaller piping bag with white buttercream to pipe on the ears, making sure to bring the ears to a point.

12 / Pipe pink buttercream for the centre of the ears and for a little nose, then pipe on eyes and a mouth using the black buttercream. Or use edible eye sprinkles for the eyes. Use black sprinkles (or more buttercream) for the whiskers. Colour extra buttercream and pipe for different accessories, or add sprinkles of your choice. Store in an airtight container for 3 days,

or in the fridge in an airtight container for up to a week. As with most cakes, this is best eaten at room temperature.

Tip: You can also pipe a buttercream cat (page 23) onto these muffins!

CAT TIP "If any of the cupcakes were overfilled or domed too much, just use a serrated knife to trim the top so that you have a flat surface to pipe me on to."

Kitty-Kat Cake

Close your eyes and picture cats playing happily and spiritedly in a pile of sweets [candies]. Isn't it just the most joyous thing?

Well... here it is: the ultimate moist chocolate cake with cats playing in sweets! It's easy to quickly whip up for a birthday celebration, and there's minimal washing-up as the cake is made in just one bowl! Kids will love sneaking their favourite sweeties from the top and trying to save the cats from being sliced along with the cake, or even just eating them before you start slicing...

Don't skip adding the boiling water at the end – this makes the batter very liquidy (don't worry though, that's normal!) and helps to dissolve the cocoa powder and incorporate it into the batter. The extra moisture also helps to produce a soft and unbelievably moist cake. The coffee granules also add a depth of flavour to the chocolate, although the actual coffee flavour will be undetectable, so don't worry if you're not a coffee fan!

DIFFICULTY 🐾 🐾, or for the Marshmeowllow Cats, 🐾 🐾 🐾 🐾 🐾
This cake looks impressive but it is actually very easy to both bake and decorate. If you want to keep the decoration on the easier side, style with 3D Cookie Cats (page 12) or Fondant or Marzipan cats (page 15). Or to make this EVEN easier, decorate with plastic cat figures/toys (just remove these before eating). If you want an extra 5-paw challenge, decorate this with Marshmeowllow Cats (page 19).

SERVES: 14–16 (MAKES 2 X 23-CM [9-IN] CAKES)

Continued overleaf

Can be made gluten-free

CAKE

softened butter, for greasing

330g [2½ cups] plain [all-purpose] flour (to make gluten-free, substitute with a gluten-free plain flour blend plus ¾ tsp xanthan gum)

430g [2 cups plus 2 Tbsp] caster or granulated sugar

100g [1 cup] unsweetened cocoa powder

2 tsp baking powder (or gluten-free baking powder)

1½ tsp bicarbonate of soda [baking soda]

1 tsp fine salt

220ml [1 cup minus 4 tsp] whole milk (or use plant-based milk if necessary)

1 Tbsp white wine vinegar

105ml [⅓ cup plus 1 Tbsp] vegetable oil (or other neutral-tasting oil)

2 medium eggs

1 Tbsp vanilla bean paste

250ml [1 cup plus 2 tsp] freshly made instant black hot coffee (or just use 250ml [1 cup] boiling water instead of coffee)

GANACHE

450g [1lb] semisweet, bittersweet or milk chocolate, finely chopped

360ml [1½ cups] double [heavy] cream (or use coconut milk)

PLUS

36 individual chocolate wafer finger bars (or similar)

around 700g [1lb 9oz] of your favourite sweets [candies] and chocolates for the top

edible cats, such as 3D Cookie Cats, Fondant or Marzipan cats, Meowringue or Marshmeowllow Cats (see pages 12–19) OR use cat figurines/toys

1 / Preheat the oven to 170°C [340°F/Gas mark 3]. Grease the base and sides of 2 x 23-cm [9-in] cake tins with butter and line the bases with a circle of baking paper.

2 / Whisk the plain flour (plus xanthan gum, if gluten-free), sugar, cocoa powder, baking powder, bicarbonate of soda and salt together in a large bowl until combined.

3 / Add the milk, vinegar, oil, eggs and vanilla and whisk again until combined. Add the hot coffee (or boiling water) and mix until everything is combined. The batter will be thin and runny – this is normal and what you want for a moist cake.

4 / Immediately divide the batter evenly between the prepared tins and bake for around 35 minutes until the cake slightly comes away from the sides of the tin and a skewer inserted into the centre comes out dry. Leave to cool in the tins for 15 minutes, then turn out onto a wire rack and peel off the baking paper. Leave to cool completely.

5 / Meanwhile, make the ganache. Place the chocolate in a large heatproof bowl. Heat the double cream in a pan on the stove until JUST starting to bubble around the edges, then immediately pour over the chocolate. Leave for 2 minutes, then stir until all the chocolate has melted. If there are still pieces of unmelted chocolate, transfer back to the pan and return to the stove. Stir over a low heat until all the chocolate has melted (or place in a microwave for very short 5–10-second bursts). When smooth, leave in the fridge for 15–30 minutes until the ganache has cooled to a spreadable consistency.

6 / Once the cakes are cool, use a serrated knife to trim off any domes on top. Place a blob of ganache on your chosen serving board, then place a layer of cake centred on top. Spread some ganache over the cake, then sandwich this with the second cake layer. Cover the top and sides generously with ganache. Press the chocolate wafer bars into the sides, covering the whole circumference of the cake. Pop the cake into the fridge (or freezer) until the ganache feels firm and wafer bars are secure. Pour your favourite colourful sweets and chocolate on top, then decorate with edible cats playing and snoozing in among the candy. Store in an airtight container at room temperature for 5 days.

CAT TIP *"For you humans who love chocolate and want an extra depth of flavour, you can add 70g [½ cup plus 2 tsp] cacao nibs to the batter before baking. These don't add any extra sweetness, but add intense bursts of pure chocolate flavour."*

Purrsian Love Cake

This cake is so moist due to the almonds and the reduced amount of flour, and it doesn't skimp on the flavour. Even several days after baking, this cake will remain as fresh and moist tasting as the day it was baked. That's if this hungry cat doesn't polish it off first…

DIFFICULTY 🐾 🐾

Can be made gluten-free

CAKE

170g [¾ cup] salted butter, softened, plus extra for greasing
170g [¾ cup plus 1½ Tbsp] caster or granulated sugar
25ml [1 Tbsp] vegetable oil
4 medium eggs
110g [¾ cup plus 1½ Tbsp] plain [all-purpose] flour (to make gluten-free, substitute with a gluten-free plain flour blend plus ¼ tsp xanthan gum)
1 tsp baking powder (or use gluten-free baking powder)
260g [2⅔ cups] ground almonds
2 tsp ground green cardamom (for the best, strongest flavour, grind these freshly from the seeds using a pestle and mortar or spice grinder. You can get the seeds from the pods, or buy packs of just the whole seeds. If using pre-ground cardamom, you may need to increase this quantity a little to achieve a stronger flavour)
finely grated zest and juice of 1 lemon
2 tsp rose water

SERVES: 10

SOAKING SYRUP

juice of 1 lemon (about 45ml [3 Tbsp])
3 Tbsp caster or granulated sugar
1 tsp rose water

ICING DRIZZLE

200g [1½ cups minus 1 Tbsp] icing [confectioners'] sugar
juice of 1 lemon (you may not need it all)

TO DECORATE

1 Tbsp roughly chopped pistachios
1 tsp edible dried rose petals
2 x 3D Cookie or Fondant/Marzipan Cats (see pages 12 or 15)

CAT FACT: Cats blink slowly at you to tell you that they love you.

Continued overleaf

1 / Preheat the oven to 160°C [325°F/Gas mark 3]. Grease the base and sides of a 23-cm [9-in] round cake tin with butter, then line the base with a circle of baking paper.

2 / Place the butter and sugar in a stand mixer fitted with a balloon whisk attachment (or use a handheld electric whisk) and cream together until very fluffy and very light in colour. Add the oil and beat again until combined.

3 / Add the eggs, one at a time, beating well after each addition.

4 / Add the flour (plus xanthan gum, if gluten-free), baking powder, ground almonds, ground cardamom, lemon zest and juice and rose water and mix until just combined.

5 / Transfer the batter to the prepared cake tin and bake for around 45 minutes, or until a skewer inserted into the centre comes out clean.

6 / Towards the end of the baking time, make the soaking syrup. Add all the ingredients to a pan over a low heat and stir until the sugar has dissolved.

7 / When the cake is baked, leave it in the tin for 5 minutes, then turn it out onto a wire rack. Using a skewer, poke holes all over the top while the cake is still warm, then drizzle with the syrup. Leave to cool.

8 / When the cake is completely cool, transfer to a serving plate. Make the icing drizzle by whisking together the icing sugar and enough lemon juice in a bowl to make a fluid but thick icing. Test it by spooning a drip on one side of the cake to make sure that it flows and settles smoothly on top within a minute, but isn't so thin that it runs off.

9 / When you're happy with your icing consistency, spoon it on top of the cake and push some of the icing off the edges so that it carefully drips down.

10 / Decorate the top with the chopped pistachios and dried rose petals, then use a spoon to carve out a piece from the side of the cake and arrange one of your cats so it looks like it has sneakily eaten some of the cake. Place another on top of the cake in the centre. You can use a little icing and make it so this one is holding some pistachios and rose petals. Play about with it to create a unique little love story. Store in an airtight container for up to a week.

Sweet Treats

Feline Like Brownies?

The best EVER brownies. Gooey, chunky and decadently chocolate-y, with a shiny crackly top. Made even more su-*purr*-rior by the additional cats and shortbread layer – and the contrasting crunch that the cookies bring to the party. There's also a secret peanut butter layer...

The cats determine the portion sizes here, so jumbo brownie portions it is.

DIFFICULTY 🐾 🐾

The main things to watch out for are making sure you have read the recipe fully to begin with, then whisking the mixture a lot before adding the flour, then mixing as minimally as possible after you add the flour. The brownies also need to be cooled properly before eating them, otherwise they'll be too runny in the centre, but there are no major cat-astrophes with this one, even if you do something slightly 'wrong' it'll pawbably still be tasty.

MAKES: ONE 23 X 23-CM [9 X 9-IN] TRAY OF BROWNIES

Can be made gluten-free

SHORTBREAD BASE AND CATS
1½ quantities of shortbread (Calico Cat Cookies, page 117)

BROWNIES
220g [1 cup minus 1 tsp] salted butter, melted, plus extra for greasing
3 Tbsp vegetable oil
200g [1 cup] soft dark brown sugar
200g [1 cup] caster or granulated sugar
4 large eggs
1 tsp vanilla bean paste
¼ tsp salt

140g [1 cup plus 1 Tbsp] plain [all-purpose] flour (to make gluten-free, substitute with a gluten-free flour blend plus ¼ tsp xanthan gum)
100g [1 cup] unsweetened cocoa powder
250g [9oz] dark [bittersweet] chocolate, roughly chopped

PEANUT BUTTER LAYER
(you can omit this if you prefer)
160g [¾ cup minus 1 tsp] smooth peanut butter
105g [¾ cup] icing [confectioners'] sugar
1 tsp vanilla bean paste
25ml [2 Tbsp] milk

Continued overleaf

"Slice AROUND the cats!"

1 / Grease and line a 23 x 23-cm [9 x 9-in] square tin, allowing the baking paper to extend up two of the sides to make lifting out easier later.

2 / First, make the shortbread following the instructions on page 117 and follow steps 1–3.

3 / Remove 250g [9oz] of the shortbread and set aside. Press the remaining shortbread into the base of the prepared tin in an even layer and chill in the fridge or freezer.

4 / With the reserved shortbread, follow steps 4–8 on page 117 to make and bake at least 9 calico cats – just pinch off half the amount of dough for the orange and brown sections, and use ¼ tsp unsweetened cocoa powder. Leave the oven on.

5 / Return your attention to the chilled shortbread layer in the tin and bake for 20 minutes. Leave to cool slightly.

6 / Meanwhile, start making the brownie mixture. Using

a handheld electric whisk, whisk the butter, salt, oil and sugars together in a large bowl until just combined. (Or use a stand mixer fitted with a balloon whisk attachment.) Add the eggs and vanilla and whisk at high speed until pale in colour. Sift in the flour (plus xanthan gum, if gluten-free) and cocoa powder and fold in. Add the roughly chopped chocolate and fold again. Avoid overmixing after adding the flour.

7 / Scoop half the batter on top of the shortbread layer and use the back of a spoon to level the top.

8 / For the peanut butter layer, using a spoon, beat the peanut butter, icing sugar, vanilla and milk together in a large bowl until thick (similar to cookie dough). Take chunks of the dough, flatten them with your hands, then place on top of the batter. Spoon and spread the remaining half of the brownie mixture on top and decorate with 9 baked calico cats.

9 / Bake for 45–60 minutes (longer baking time for a slightly less gooey brownie) until there is no longer any liquid in the middle, but it still should look technically 'undercooked' – as it will finish cooking as it cools. Leave to cool in the oven for 30 minutes, then set the tin on the work surface and leave to cool at room temperature. To help speed up cooling, you can put the tin into the freezer. Once it's fully cool it should be set and can be lifted out of the tin (using the baking paper 'handles' to help).

Tip: Feel free to snack on a corner before they finish cooling! The corners will always be slightly firmer than the centre.

10 / Once cool, peel off the baking paper and slice into 9 segments, being careful not to slice up any of the kitties! Eat straight away or store in an airtight container for up to a week. You can also successfully freeze these if suitably wrapped.

Mochi Cats

One of my two cats is called Mochi, so to make a mochi cat was a de-*fur*-nite must! The wonderfully chewy skin paired with the smooth ice cream is a texture combination that leaves you coming back to the freezer to have more and more.

DIFFICULTY 🐾 🐾, if using a solid filling, or 🐾 🐾 🐾 🐾
This one is trickier purely because of the use of ice cream, so you need to work fast and to decorate! But making the mochi skin is surprisingly simple, so if you want to make these easier (🐾 🐾), then fill these with a more solid filling, such as sweet red or black bean paste, cookie dough, thick pastry cream, fresh fruit, etc. There are many options for different fillings. You can even eat these plain, without any filling!

MAKES: 10 (MEDIUM CATS, BUT YOU CAN VARY THE SIZES AND PLAY ABOUT WITH THIS!)

Can be made vegan and naturally gluten-free

10 small portions of ice cream of your choice (each portion about 1 Tbsp)
flaked [slivered] almonds, around 2 per cat
160g [1 cup] glutinous rice flour, plus extra for sprinkling (or use cornflour [cornstarch] for sprinkling)
65g [⅓ cup plus 1 tsp] caster or granulated sugar
220ml [1 cup minus 1 Tbsp] water
gel food dye colours of your choice mixed with a tiny amount of water

> **CAT TIP** *"You can make me different sizes! Use an 8-cm [3¼-in] circle of mochi skin to wrap ½ Tbsp of ice cream and make me as a kitten. Or make me chonky by using a 12-cm [4½-in] cutter for 1½ Tbsp ice cream."*

Continued overleaf

"If it's a very hot day, you should take a cat nap and make me when it's more chill."

1 / First, create 10 small and roughly oblong scoops of ice cream, about 1 Tbsp each, then place on a sheet of baking paper and return to the freezer. Use a sharp knife to cut the almonds so that they are a little pointier.

2 / Next, make the mochi skin. Add the glutinous rice flour, sugar and water to a microwaveable bowl and whisk by hand until combined. Cover with plastic wrap and microwave on high for 1 minute. Remove from the microwave and whisk. It will still be very liquid at this point so won't be too difficult to mix. Cover again and heat for another 30 seconds. It will be thicker/lumpier now; whisk again and return to the microwave. Keep heating in 30-second bursts and whisking or stirring after each. When the mixture becomes thick, switch to stirring with a spatula, otherwise it will just clump inside

the whisk. After a total of about 4–5 minutes, the dough should look slightly translucent and be very sticky and thickened.

3 / Sprinkle a very generous amount of glutinous rice flour or cornflour onto a work surface, then scoop the mochi on top (careful! It will be very hot). Sprinkle more rice flour on top. Carefully roll out to about 5mm [¼in] thick while checking that it isn't sticking to your surface (if so, use more flour). Leave to cool for about 15–30 minutes.

4 / Once cool, cut out a circle using a 7.5-cm [3-in] cutter. Brush off the excess rice flour on top, then place a scoop of ice cream in the centre. Lift the edges of the dough to encase the ice cream, then press together at the top to seal. You need to work quickly to avoid the ice cream melting. Very quickly press in the prepared nuts for the ears. Once done, immediately wrap in plastic

wrap (to help it keep its shape) and place in the freezer to firm up. Don't worry if a little ice cream seeps out, this will harden when chilled in the freezer. Repeat to make all the mochi ice creams.

Tip: The ice cream will want to melt fast when near your warm hands, so you can wear gloves to help prevent the heat transferring. It also helps to work near the freezer.

5 / Once the mochi ice creams have firmed up, paint the backs of the mochi with gel food dye colours of your choice, mixed with a little water. Then paint on a little face to bring the mochi cats to life.

6 / Place in an airtight container and keep in the freezer for up to 2 weeks until ready to snack on.

Pavlov's Cat

Unlike Pavlov's famous dog, Pavlov's cats do what they want, when they want – including sleeping in cosy and delicious meringue clouds, nestling in among the smooth cream, tangy lemon curd and sweet fruit.

DIFFICULTY ❀ ❀ ❀ or, if piping, ❀ ❀ ❀ ❀
The higher rating is for piping the *Meowringue Cats* (page 16), but if you want to make this easier then top this pavlova with some scruffy *Meowringue Cats* (see tip on page 10).

SERVES: 10

Naturally gluten-free and can be made vegan

PAVLOVA AND MEOWRINGUE CATS
2 quantities meringue mix from page 16 (use 8 egg whites and 520g [3¾ cups] icing [confectioners'] sugar)

LEMON CURD (OPTIONAL)
(to make this vegan, omit the curd or use your favourite vegan lemon curd recipe; this makes more than needed for the pavlova, just in order to use up all the egg yolks, but you can store the extra curd in an airtight jar in the fridge to enjoy for 1–2 weeks. Sterilize the jar to ensure that it lasts longer!)
finely grated zest and juice of 5 medium lemons
8 medium egg yolks (leftover from the pavlova)
200g [1 cup] caster or granulated sugar
60g [5 Tbsp] salted butter

TO ASSEMBLE
500ml [2 cups plus 2 Tbsp] double [heavy] cream (or use your favourite whippable vegan cream)
1 Tbsp vanilla bean paste
250g [2½ cups] fresh strawberries, sliced
250g [2 cups] fresh raspberries
2 kiwi fruit, peeled and sliced

CAT TIP *Use whatever fruit and berries you have lying around the house!*

Continued overleaf

1 / Preheat the oven to 80°C [176°F/Gas mark ¼]. Line 2 large baking sheets with baking paper or silicone mats. To help guide you later, draw 3 separate 18-cm [7-in] circles (2 on one sheet and 1 on the other), then flip the papers over so the marked lines are on the underneath but still visible.

2 / Follow steps 1–4 on page 16 to make the meringue, but make double the quantity. Make sure to set the egg yolks aside to make the lemon curd later.

3 / Set about a fifth of the meringue aside, then spoon the remaining meringue into the middle of the circles on the prepared baking sheets, dividing the meringue equally between each. Use the back of a spoon to spread the meringue out to the edge of the circles and level it. Using the reserved meringue, follow steps 5–7 on page 16 to make various meringue cats. Pipe these onto any spaces left around the meringue circles.

4 / Bake for around 2 hours, then switch the oven off and leave the meringue in the oven to cool for at least 30 minutes (or overnight if you have time!). You can take the meringue cats out sooner, but they won't be affected if you leave them in longer. This is because meringues are 'baked' at a very low temperature as the intention is to dry out the meringues rather than bake

them in the same way as a cake. The meringues are ready when they are dry underneath and you can lift them off the baking paper.

5 / Meanwhile, make the lemon curd. Put the lemon juice, zest, reserved egg yolks and sugar into a heatproof bowl set over a pan of simmering water, making sure the bottom of the bowl doesn't touch the water. Stir constantly for about 15 minutes. The mixture will gradually thicken. When it thickly coats the back of a spoon, add the butter and stir in until melted. Transfer to a bowl or jar, cover with plastic wrap and leave to chill in the fridge.

6 / When you're ready to serve, whip the cream with the vanilla bean paste to soft peaks. Place one layer of meringue on a serving plate and spoon the cream on top. Swirl through a generous amount of lemon curd. If the curd is too thick from being refrigerated for a long time, just whisk in a little lemon juice to thin. Scatter with fresh fruit and place the second layer of meringue on top. Spoon more curd over, letting some drip down the sides. Repeat, placing the final layer on top and decorating with more cream, lemon curd, fresh fruit and some carefully placed meringue cats among the fruit. Best eaten straight away, although it will be fine overnight in the fridge.

Pavlov's Kittens

You thought there couldn't be anything cuter than Pavlov's Cat (page 72), but yes, somehow these are even more adorable baby kitten versions. If you wanted to make these for a big party, you could even make a large Pavlov's Cat which could be surrounded by its baby Pavlov's Kittens!

DIFFICULTY 🐾 🐾 🐾

Naturally gluten-free and can be made vegan

MINI PAVLOVAS
1 quantity meringue mix (see Meowringue Cats on page 16)

LEMON CURD (OPTIONAL)
(to make this vegan, omit the curd, or use your favourite vegan lemon curd recipe)
½ quantity Lemon Curd (page 72)

MAKES: 8

TO ASSEMBLE
250ml [1 cup] double [heavy] cream
½ Tbsp vanilla bean paste
fresh berries, sliced
black gel food dye mixed with a tiny amount of water or Quick Black Icing (page 12)

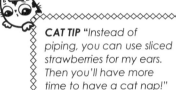

CAT TIP *"Instead of piping, you can use sliced strawberries for my ears. Then you'll have more time to have a cat nap!"*

1 / Preheat the oven to 80°C [176°F/Gas mark ¼]. Line a large baking sheet with baking paper.

2 / Follow steps 1–4 on page 16 to make the meringue. Make sure to set the egg yolks aside to make the lemon curd later. If want to make mini pavlovas of different colours, divide the meringue between different bowls and stir through food dye to colour.

3 / Spoon 8 tablespoons of meringue onto the baking paper, then use the back of a spoon and drag this upwards all around the sides of the meringue to shape it and create the pattern around the sides. You can hold a second spoon in the centre of the mini pavlova to help with creating the structure.

4 / Put a small amount of meringue into a piping [pastry] bag and cut a small tip or ensure it has a small round piping tip attached. Pipe 16 cat ear shapes onto the baking paper, in the gaps. You could also pipe bow ties and other trinkets to accessorize your cats!

5 / Bake for around 1 hour 30 minutes, then switch off the oven and leave the meringue in the oven to cool for at least 30 minutes (or overnight if you have time!). They are ready when they are dry underneath and peel off the baking paper easily.

6 / Meanwhile, make the lemon curd following step 5 on page 74.

7 / When you're ready to serve, place the meringues on a serving plate(s), then spoon a little lemon curd into the centre of each mini pavlova.

Tip: If the curd is too thick from being refrigerated for a long time, just whisk in a little lemon juice to thin.

8 / Whip the cream with the vanilla bean paste to soft peaks. Spoon it on top of the mini pavlovas, add the cat ears, then decorate with small pieces of fresh fruit.

9 / Paint the facial features using black food dye mixed with a tiny amount of water, or make the black icing following step 6 on page 14 and use this to pipe on facial details.

Meowgical Purrmaid Tang Yuan

If you like mochi, you will love *tang yuan*. It's got that similar addictive chew once boiled, and can also be filled, although many people (including me!) enjoy it without any filling. The sweetness comes mostly from the broth, and it's all about the chew. They are also very tactile and enjoyable to shape, as the dough is similar to playdough; therefore, it's easy to construct shapes as it doesn't stick to your fingers but sticks well to itself when you need to stick together the tail, head or ears!

And a little secret: these *Purrmaid tang yuan* look adorable, but they are EXTRA adorable and joyful once you add them to the broth, because of the swishiness of their tails while they're in the water. Yes – *FUR*-REAL, their tails MOVE! You've got to make them to see!

Try making your own different versions of these cat tang yuan! You could even make fish-shaped ones to accompany them!

DIFFICULTY 🐾 🐾

The dough takes 10 minutes to make and it's actually difficult to go wrong! The extra difficulty is due to the shaping, but all cats are cute so whatever you do it will look good, so just go for it!

SERVES: 3

Naturally vegan and gluten-free

TANG YUAN DOUGH
130g [1 cup] glutinous rice flour
25g [2¾ Tbsp] icing [confectioners'] sugar
4 Tbsp (60g) boiling water
4 Tbsp (60g) room temperature water
pink, orange, green and black gel food dyes (or use your favourite colours)

FILLING
(optional, and double this quantity if you also want to fill the purrmaid-shaped tang yuan*!)*
15g [1¾ Tbsp] roasted black sesame seeds (you can buy these already roasted, or toast them yourself in a frying pan [skillet] over a low heat)
15g [1¾ Tbsp] icing [confectioners'] sugar
10g [2 tsp] butter, softened (or vegan butter – use one that's close to 80% fat content)

BROTH
1 litre [4 cups plus 3 Tbsp] water
200g [1 cup] caster or granulated sugar
knotted pandan leaf (optional; swap this with 1 tsp vanilla extract if you don't have pandan leaf)
3 Tbsp blue spirulina powder, or a tiny drop of blue food dye

CAT TIPS *"We're only half mermaid, so we will only float in boiling water. To make us look our best, serve us in shallow soup bowls so we can rest on the bottom."*

"Also, 'glutinous rice flour' deceptively sounds like it contains gluten, but it doesn't. The name comes from its glue-like consistency when cooked."

Continued overleaf

1 / For the filling (if making), grind the sesame seeds and icing sugar in a food processor until they turn into a paste. Add the soft butter and mix with a spoon until combined. Chill in the fridge for 15–30 minutes until firm enough to handle. Divide the filling into pea-sized balls, then chill in the fridge.

2 / To make the dough, add the glutinous rice flour and icing sugar to a medium heatproof bowl and stir to combine, then, while stirring, pour over the boiling water. Add the room temperature water, 1 Tbsp at a time, using a spoon to mix in.

3 / Turn the mixture out onto a work surface and knead by hand until the dough is smooth and soft. It should feel like playdough – not sticky but not dry or easily cracking either. If it's too dry, just knead in a little more water until smooth.

4 / Pinch off a pea-sized piece of dough, and knead in some food dye to colour this pink. Pinch off a marble-sized piece of dough (or 7g [⅛oz]), and knead orange food dye into this. Divide the remaining dough into 2 and knead in green food dye into one piece, leaving the other piece white. If it's too sticky, knead in a little extra glutinous rice flour.

5 / Shape a piece of green dough into the mermaid's tail (you can marble it with a little white dough, if you like), then firmly press on 2 small pieces for the end of the tail. Make a round shape for the head using white dough, then add triangular ear shapes, using your hand to push and press to make sure they stick. Add orange dough to add an extra colour dimension – just use a thin piece of this and thinly spread or pat and blend out over the white dough where you want it, then you can add some orange ears too. Press the head onto the tail so it's sticking firmly. Add a little nose using the pink dough, and arms using the white dough. Paint the face using black food dye mixed with the tiniest amount of water. Make 6 purrmaid shapes in total.

6 / Using the remaining dough, combine random bits of different colours, then press out into circles, trying to make the sides thin but the middle thicker. Place a small piece of black sesame filling (if using) in the centre of each, then close up the dough, pinch the seams firmly and roll into a ball.

Tip: You can also fill the purrmaid-shaped tang yuan; just use a small amount of filling and do this carefully when shaping the head and/or tail!

7 / Bring a large pan of water to a gentle boil, then add all the shaped tang yuan dough (purrmaids and balls), giving them a little push at first to stop them sticking to the bottom. You know they are cooked once they float to the top. The balls will cook quickly in around 5 minutes, and the purrmaid shapes will take around 10 or more minutes as they are larger.

8 / Meanwhile for the broth, in another saucepan, add the water, sugar and knotted pandan leaf (if using). Simmer for about 15 minutes, then add the blue spirulina and whisk in until dissolved. If using vanilla extract, add it at this point. Divide the soup between 3 serving bowls. When the purrmaids and balls are ready, divide them among the serving bowls and enjoy straight away.

CAT TIP *"Gentle boil and not too rapid, otherwise my mermaid tail can get damaged!"*

Creme Puff Honey Cats

This choux pastry is light and crisp all at the same time and filled with a cat-tified dollop of silky honey cream. Choux pastry can be seen as a finicky bake, but just as is the case with finicky cats, you just have to follow its rules and don't rush into things – and only then will you be rewarded with cuteness.

Make a *meow*ntain of these to snack on (as they are an incredible snack even unfilled), then decorate around half of them as cats with cream!

DIFFICULTY 🐾 🐾 🐾

MAKES: AROUND 30–40 CHOUX AU CRAQUELIN BUNS

Can be made gluten-free

CHOUX
85g [⅓ cup plus 2 tsp] unsalted butter
225ml [1 cup minus 1 Tbsp] water
pinch of salt
50g [⅓ cup plus 1 Tbsp] strong white flour
50g [⅓ cup plus 1 Tbsp] plain [all-purpose] flour (to make gluten-free, substitute both the plain and strong flours for 100g [¾ cup] of a gluten-free flour blend – don't add xanthan gum)
3 medium eggs

CRAQUELIN
75g [½ cup plus 1 Tbsp] unsalted butter
75g [⅓ cup plus 2 tsp] light muscovado sugar
75g [½ cup plus 1 Tbsp] plain [all-purpose] flour (to make gluten-free, substitute for 75g [½ cup plus 1 Tbsp] of a gluten-free flour blend and a pinch of xanthan gum)

HONEY WHIPPED CREAM FILLING
400ml [2 cups minus 2 Tbsp] double [heavy] cream
3 Tbsp honey
1 Tbsp vanilla bean paste
yellow and black gel food dyes
flaked [slivered] almonds

Continued overleaf

CAT FACT: Creme Puff is the name of the oldest cat ever recorded, living to a grand old age of 38 years and 3 days!

1 / Preheat the oven to 220°C [425°F/Gas mark 7]. Line 2 large baking sheets with baking paper or silicone mats.

2 / Make the choux. Chop the butter into cubes and add it to a small saucepan with the water and salt. Heat until the butter has melted and the mixture is starting to bubble. Meanwhile, combine both flours in a separate bowl. When the butter mixture is bubbling, remove it from the heat and add the flour all in one go. Stir with a wooden spoon until it forms a smooth ball that pulls away from the sides very easily.

3 / Transfer the mixture to a large bowl. Leave to cool for 5–10 minutes. You can mix it on low speed to help cool it down faster.

4 / Meanwhile, make the craquelin. Beat the butter and sugar together in a large bowl with a spoon until combined and spreadable. Add the flour (plus xanthan gum, if gluten-free) and stir to form a ball. Roll out between 2 sheets of plastic wrap and transfer to the freezer.

5 / Return to the cooled choux mixture, adding two of the eggs, one at a time, whisking after each addition until combined. Whisk the third egg in a separate bowl and gradually add 1 Tbsp at a time, mixing well after each addition. You are looking for a glossy consistency that leaves a 'v' shape when a spoon is lifted out of the dough. You may not need all of the third egg.

6 / Transfer the choux pastry to a piping [pastry] bag and cut a large tip or use a large piping tip. Pipe 3.5-cm [1½-in] blobs onto the prepared baking sheet, holding your piping bag perpendicular to the sheet and squeezing in one place. Remove the craquelin from the freezer and stamp out 3-cm [1¼-in] circles to fit on top of each piped choux. Place a circle of craquelin on top of each one.

7 / Bake for 10 minutes, then reduce the oven temperature to 180°C [350°F/Gas mark 4] and bake for a further 15–20 minutes. Don't open the oven during baking, to avoid the choux deflating. When the choux have finished baking, immediately turn them over and use a knife to pierce the base. This is so that the air inside has somewhere to escape. Leave to cool.

8 / Meanwhile, make the honey whipped cream filling. Add the cream, honey and vanilla to a large bowl and whip until soft peaks form. Be careful not to overwhip, as it will end up getting overworked as you transfer it to the piping bag and pipe. While whipping, gradually add very small amounts of food dye until a pale yellow colour is achieved.

9 / Transfer around a quarter of the whipped cream to a piping bag and cut a large tip or use a large piping tip. Place a small amount of whipped cream into a second piping bag and cut a small tip or use a small piping tip. Cut the tops off each choux bun, fill with a mound of

piped whipped cream using the larger bag, then use the small piping bag to add paws.

10 / Place a small piece of slivered almond for the nose/mouth area and insert small slivered almonds for the ears. You can use a small sharp knife to cut these so they are pointier and more cat-like.

11 / Place the reserved choux lids back on top, then draw facial details onto the filling using a cocktail stick [toothpick] dipped into a very small amount of black food dye. Use a VERY minimal amount otherwise your cats will have big black and dripping eyes! These are best eaten the same day they are made. The black food dye will bleed into the cream once refrigerated, so it's best to serve these straight away after decorating.

CAT TIP Don't fill the piping bag too full of cream as the cream at the top will end up overwhipped due to the squeezing action from your hand.

Pecan Peekin' Cat Tart

Every bake is better with cats. How could anyone resist cats peeking out from pecans in a pie? To make sure your pastry base is beautifully crisp and never soggy, keep it chilled and don't skip the blind baking.

DIFFICULTY 🐾 🐾 🐾

SERVES: AROUND 8–10 (MAKES 1 SHARING-SIZED TART, 22CM (8½IN) IN DIAMETER, 3CM [1¼IN] HIGH)

Can be made vegan and/or gluten free

PASTRY
(or use store-bought pastry)
200g [1½ cups] plain [all-purpose] flour, plus extra (to make gluten-free, substitute with a gluten-free plain flour blend plus 1¼ tsp xanthan gum)
110g [½ cup minus ¼ Tbsp] salted butter, cold, cubed, plus extra for greasing (or vegan butter – use one that's close to 80% fat content)

30g [2 Tbsp] caster or granulated sugar
around 2 Tbsp iced water (if making this gluten-free, egg white or aquafaba will give the pastry more binding strength)

PECAN FILLING
60g [¼ cup] unsalted butter
110g [⅓ cup] golden [light corn] syrup
1 Tbsp vanilla bean paste
140g [¾ cup minus 2 tsp] soft light brown sugar
¼ tsp salt
2 medium eggs

1½ Tbsp bourbon (or use fresh orange juice)
150g [1⅓ cups] pecans (70g [⅔ cup] whole and 80g [¾ cup] chopped)

PLUS
gel food dyes
1 egg (or 2 Tbsp aquafaba)
cream or ice cream, to serve

1 / Grease a 22-cm [8½-in] x 3-cm [1¼-in] high loose-bottomed tart tin with butter, and line a baking sheet with baking paper.

2 / Add the flour (plus xanthan gum, if gluten-free) and butter to a large bowl, then rub the butter into the flour until it resembles fine breadcrumbs. Don't overwork. Stir in the caster sugar. Gradually stir in enough iced water to combine the pastry into a smooth ball.

3 / Roll out the pastry on a well-floured surface to a large circle, about 3mm (⅛ in) thick. Carefully lift and drape the pastry over the tin, then gently press the pastry into the edges of the tin and trim off the top edge. Prick the base a few times with a fork. Set aside the pastry trimmings.

Tip: Don't stretch the pastry when moulding it to the tin; gently lift and drape/guide it into place. Stretching it will result in too much shrinking after baking!

4 / Chill the tart shell in the fridge for at least 30 minutes.

5 / Meanwhile, preheat the oven to 180°C [350°F/Gas mark 4]. Reroll the remaining pastry, then use a cutter to create cat shapes of different sizes and transfer to the prepared baking sheet. Separate the egg and lightly beat the yolk, then paint the cats using food dye mixed with some of the yolk to dilute. The addition of egg creates a sheen after the pastry has been baked, so it looks almost like

Continued overleaf

edible pottery. The more you use, the more sheen you will notice. You want to paint cute varied markings and different types of cats! Chill in the fridge or freezer for around 20 minutes, along with the tart.

If making vegan, use aquafaba – this will still give a slight sheen but not as much as egg yolk.

6 / When the tart shell is chilled, cover it with foil, moulding this to fit the shape of the tart and covering all the pastry. Fill with baking beans [pie weights] (or rice or lentils), making sure they spread into all the edges. Place on a baking sheet and blind bake for 15 minutes, then remove the foil and baking beans. Brush the base and sides with a little beaten egg white (or aquafaba) from earlier – this will help keep it crisper after adding the filling later. Bake for a further 10 minutes until the pastry is lightly golden all over. Leave to cool completely.

7 / Bake the chilled cat pastry shapes for 8–12 minutes (the bigger your cat shapes, the longer they take to bake), or until they are very lightly coloured at the edges. Leave to cool on the sheet for 5 minutes, then transfer to a wire rack to finish cooling.

8 / Reduce the oven temperature to 150°C [300°F/ Gas mark 2]. Make the filling. Melt the butter in the microwave in 10-second bursts, then leave to cool. Add the golden syrup, vanilla, light brown sugar, salt, eggs, bourbon (or fresh orange juice) and cooled melted butter to a large bowl and whisk with a balloon whisk until combined.

9 / Sprinkle the chopped pecans in an even layer over the cooled pastry base, then pour the filling on top, close to the brim. Arrange the whole pecans in a ring around the outside circumference.

10 / Bake for 35–40 minutes until the filling is puffed around the edge and the centre is set but with a slight wobble. Remove from the oven, then leave to cool at room temperature before chilling in the fridge for at least 2 hours. Once cool, insert the pastry cats, then serve with cream or ice cream. Keep covered in the fridge for up to a week.

Vegan filling alternative:

65g [¼ cup plus 1 tsp] unsalted vegan butter – use one that's close to 80% fat content
100g [⅓ cup] golden [light corn] syrup
1 Tbsp vanilla bean paste
155g [¾ cup] soft light brown sugar
¼ tsp salt
60ml [¼ cup] coconut milk
3 Tbsp cornflour [cornstarch]
1½ Tbsp bourbon (or use fresh orange juice)
150g [1⅓ cups] pecans (70g [⅔ cup] whole and 80g [¾ cup] chopped)

1 / Make the pastry with the vegan (and/or gluten-free) substitutes listed on page 85. Mix together all the ingredients for the filling in the same way; adding coconut milk instead of the eggs.

2 / Bake for 35–40 minutes, or until puffed up at the edges but still until wobbly. Unlike the egg based version, this version remains quite liquid-y until chilled properly.

3 / Leave to cool at room temperature, then place in the fridge to chill for at least 4 hours, or until chilled throughout.

4 / Unmould, decorate and serve chilled with your favourite vegan cream or ice cream.

Psychedelic Kitty Pop Tarts

Oh no! These kitties have had way too much catnip, and have somehow ended up on your pop tarts! Delicious and buttery pop tarts that is… no wonder they landed on them.

DIFFICULTY 🐾 🐾

Can be made vegan and/or gluten-free

PASTRY

225g [1¾ cups] plain [all-purpose] flour, plus extra for dusting (to make gluten-free, substitute with a gluten-free plain flour blend plus 1½ tsp xanthan gum)

135g [⅔ cup minus 1 Tbsp] cold salted butter, cubed (or vegan butter – use one that's close to 80% fat content)

40g [3¼ Tbsp] caster or granulated sugar

2½–3 Tbsp beaten egg (from ½ medium egg) (or use aquafaba)

MAKES: 8

FILLING
12 tsp favourite jam or spread

WATER ICING
200g [1½ cups minus 1 Tbsp] icing [confectioners'] sugar, plus extra to decorate or as needed
40ml [2⅔ Tbsp] water

PLUS
pink and green gel food dyes (or use your favourite colours)
black gel food dye

CAT TIP "To make my rectangular shape with ears, you can make a quick template which you'll cut the pastry around. Place a (approx) 5.5 x 8.5-cm [2¼ x 3¼-in] rectangular cutter (or similar) on a piece of paper or card, draw around, then simply draw on ear shapes and cut around the whole shape."

Continued overleaf

1 / Line 1–2 large baking sheets with baking paper. First, make the pastry. Add the flour (plus xanthan gum, if gluten-free) to a large bowl. Add the butter and rub it into the flour until it resembles fine breadcrumbs. Don't overwork. Stir in the caster sugar. Add 2 Tbsp beaten egg to the bowl and beat with a fork, gradually combining it with the rest of the mixture (add more egg if needed). Use your hands to form the pastry into a ball. (if it's a hot day, wrap the pastry in plastic wrap and pop in the fridge for 15 minutes to chill. (This will make the pastry easier to roll out.)

2 / Roll out the pastry on a well-floured surface, about 3mm (⅛ in) thick. Place your template (see the tip on page 87) on the pastry and cut around this with a sharp knife. Repeat to cut out 20 cat shapes. You will need to reroll the pastry to use it all up.

3 / To create each pop tart, spoon 1½ tsp of your preferred filling into the centre of a rectangle, then wet the edges with a very small amount of water and place a second rectangle on top. Press the edges together to seal, then use the back of a fork to press together and ensure a good tight seal, all around. Poke 2

little holes in the top of each pastry, to allow air inside to escape. Arrange on the prepared baking sheet(s) and chill the pop tarts in the fridge for 30 minutes, or the freezer for 10 minutes. Meanwhile, preheat the oven to 180°C [350°F/Gas mark 4].

4 / Once the pop tarts are chilled, bake for about 15 minutes, or until golden. Leave to cool on the sheet(s) for 10 minutes, then transfer to a wire rack to finish cooling completely.

5 / Meanwhile, make the icing [frosting]. Add the icing sugar and water to a bowl, then whisk until smooth and combined. You are looking for a consistency that holds a trail for 10 seconds before smoothing itself out. If the icing is too runny or too thick, whisk in a very small amount of water or icing sugar to adjust. Divide the icing between different bowls (depending on how many different colours you want to make) and stir in food dye to colour each a different shade of your chosen colour(s).

6 / When the tarts are completely cool, spoon over the icing from different bowls so that the different shades look randomly swirled together. You can use the back of a spoon

to gently push different colours around and make the icing go roughly where you want it to, but you want to create drips and a random look. Leave the icing to semi-set and form a slight crust on top. You should be able to touch the icing lightly and it doesn't stick to your fingers.

7 / Add black food dye to a little leftover icing in a bowl, plus whisk in a little extra icing sugar to make it a thicker consistency, then transfer to a piping [pastry] bag. Cut a small tip (or fit with a small piping tip) and pipe on a confused looking cat face. Store in an airtight container for up to 5 days, or in the fridge for 1½ weeks, or freeze. Enjoy cold, microwave or (ideally) reheat in an oven preheated to 180°C [350°F/Gas mark 4] for 5–10 minutes. These homemade pop tarts are much more buttery and delicate than store-bought ones, so if you put them in the toaster, crumbs can flake off and end up burning, so it's best to reheat these in the oven.

CAT TIP *"Try out lots of different fillings! Chocolate spread, biscoff, jams, ganache… there are so many delicious options!"*

"Am I a cat... or a pop tart?"

Kit-Tea Scones

These are the *meowst* fluffy, soft and comforting scones. Whether you're *cat*-egorically cream first or jam first, or whether you just don't care either way, these tasty and adorable scones will make you smile. Serve with a piping hot pot of tea, clotted cream and jam – and invite your *fur*-ends.

DIFFICULTY 🐾
Could be pushing 2 paws if you include the decoration, but other than the decorating, scones are one of the easiest bakes you can make.

MAKES: AROUND 9 MEDIUM (5.5-CM [2¼-IN]) SCONES, BUT YOU CAN MIX UP THE SIZES AND MAKE A LITTLE MORE OR A LITTLE LESS

Can be made vegan and/or gluten free

350g [2⅔ cups] self-raising flour (or use a gluten-free self-raising flour blend plus ¼ tsp xanthan gum), plus extra for dusting
1 tsp baking powder (or use gluten-free baking powder)
4 Tbsp caster or granulated sugar
60g [¼ cup] salted butter, cubed and cold (or vegan butter – use one that's close to 80% fat content. If making gluten-free or gluten-free/vegan scones, increase the amount of butter to 80g [⅓ cup plus 1 tsp])
tea leaves from 2 Earl Grey tea bags

30ml [2 Tbsp] boiling water
140ml [⅔ cup minus 2 tsp] cold milk (or use any plant-based milk)
1 tsp vanilla bean paste or extract (optional)
1 Tbsp lemon juice

TO GLAZE
beaten egg (or use 4 parts plant-based milk to 1 part golden [light corn] syrup, or any other liquid sugar, such as maple syrup)

TO DECORATE
whole blanched almonds, for ears
½ quantity Royal Icing (page 127)
pink and black gel food dyes

TO SERVE
a cup of tea, clotted cream (or substitute with your favourite vegan alternative) and your favourite jam

"It's cream first."

"ACTUALLY it's jam first."

Continued overleaf

1 / Add the flour (plus xanthan gum, if gluten-free), baking powder and caster sugar to a large bowl. Add the cold butter cubes to the bowl and use your fingertips to rub them in until the mixture resembles fine breadcrumbs.

2 / Add the tea leaves to the boiling water and leave to brew for 4 minutes, then stir in the cold milk. Stir in the vanilla (if using) and lemon juice and set aside for 5 minutes.

3 / Stir the liquid into the flour mixture, then use a spoon to mix roughly. Use your hands to combine into a slightly sticky ball of dough, working the dough as minimally as possible. Dust a work surface with flour, then place the dough on top and pat it out to around 2.5cm [1in] thick. Use a 5.5-cm [2¼-in] round cutter to stamp out circles (though you can vary it and create different

sizes too!), aiming to push the cutter straight down without twisting. You will need to press what's left of the dough back together, then stamp out more. Place on a plate and leave to chill in the fridge for at least 30 minutes, or in the freezer for 10 minutes.

4 / Meanwhile, preheat the oven to 200°C [400°F/Gas mark 6] and place a large baking sheet in the oven to heat up.

5 / Brush the tops of the scones with beaten egg (or vegan substitute), then place a sheet of baking paper on the hot baking sheet and quickly but carefully arrange the scones on top.

6 / Bake for 10–15 minutes (bigger scones will take longer), or until risen and golden on top. Transfer to a wire rack and leave to cool.

7 / Insert almonds for the cat ears. Make the royal icing following the instructions on page 129, then put a third into a piping [pastry] bag. Colour 1 tsp of the remaining icing with pink food dye and put in a separate piping bag. Colour the remaining icing using black food dye and put this in a third piping bag. Cut small tips on all of these and use to pipe on the face. Start with the white mouth/nose area, then leave this to semi-set before piping the black nose and mouth on top. Pipe on eyes, whiskers, pink 'blush' and any additional details to create some unique kitties. The colours suggested here are just ideas, you can customize them however you wish! Store in an airtight container for up to 3 days, or in the fridge for 1 week, or freeze.

CAT TIP *"You don't have to use a preheated baking sheet, but this little trick will help give us an extra rise!"*

- SWEET TREATS -

Secret Kitten Hot Chocolate Bombe Surprise!

Ever wanted to melt a ball of chocolate and see a kitten emerge from it? Well, this bake means you can do exactly that! And it makes for an incredible homemade gift that will make any cat lover smile. It also happens to make the most delicious and rich hot chocolate, thanks to real chocolate melting with your milk.

NOTE: It's best to temper your chocolate for these bombes, because if your chocolate is melted without tempering then it will take a long time to set, and it will be sticky and flexible rather than snap. The main issue is that it will be difficult to stick the 2 halves together as it will be melting from your warm fingers. Tempered chocolate cocoa bombes are also great for Christmas gifts, whereas untempered ones must be kept chilled or else they will go soft.

DIFFICULTY 🐾 🐾 🐾 🐾 🐾

MAKES: 12

Can be made vegan and naturally gluten-free

CHOCOLATE FOR TEMPERING

400g [14oz] good-quality dark [bittersweet] chocolate that doesn't contain vegetable oil, finely chopped

It's easiest to work with this larger quantity when tempering, as smaller amounts will experience quicker temperature changes! Feel free to make a larger quantity, and any leftover chocolate can always be re-melted and reused later!

FILLING (PER BOMBE)

1 flat tsp unsweetened cocoa powder, plus extra for filling
1–2½ tsp caster or granulated sugar (depending on your taste), plus extra for filling

PLUS

Marshmeowllow Cats (page 19) (we all love a chonky cat, but make sure to pipe these small enough so they fit in the chocolate spheres!)
to make these vegan – use scissors to cut ear shapes into store-bought vegan marshmallows (or see tip, right)
additional add-ins you would like, such as sprinkles, sweets [candies], chocolate chips (optional)
a little white chocolate, melted, for drizzling or piping on top (optional)
½ cup hot milk per serving

> **CAT TIP** *This recipe has a high difficulty level, mostly due to the marshmallow piping. See the tip on page 19 for an easier way to make them using shop-bought marshmallows.*

Continued overleaf

1 / First, you will need to set up a bain-marie: sit a heatproof bowl (which is clean and completely dry) over a pan of boiling water (making sure the bottom of the bowl does not touch the water).

2 / Place three-quarters of the finely chopped chocolate in the heatproof bowl, and set aside a quarter of the chocolate for later. Stir the chocolate until it has melted and its temperature is 46°C [115°F] (you will need a thermometer). Start taking the chocolate off the heat before it reaches the desired temperature, because you will find that the temperature suddenly shoots up from the bowl, getting very hot.

Tip: If you pre-fur, you can also temper the chocolate in the microwave. Place the chocolate in a microwaveable bowl, and heat in 15–30-second bursts, stirring well after each until the chocolate has melted and its temperature is at 46°C [115°F], then follow step 3.

3 / Add the remaining chunks of chocolate to the bowl, while stirring constantly. Keep stirring until the temperature comes down to 32°C [90°F]. Now your chocolate is tempered and ready to use. You can check it is tempered by leaving some to set on the back of a spoon. It should set within 5 minutes. You can keep the chocolate slightly warm (but not beyond the tempered temperature) in the bain-marie for a while, so you can use it when needed.

Tip: If you find that it's taking too long for the temperature to come down to 32°C [90°F], sit the bowl of chocolate in a large bowl of cold water (being careful not to let any water touch the chocolate, as it will seize and become unusable).

4 / Spoon the tempered chocolate into 7-cm [2¾-in] diameter chocolate moulds (silicone, metal or plastic) and use a spoon to spread it around the sides to coat. Turn the moulds upside down and shake to remove any excess chocolate (you don't want the shell to be so thick that you can't fit the marshmallow cat in!). Chill in the freezer for about 5 minutes or until set, then peel the chocolate from the silicone moulds – they should come out very easily once set.

Tip: Marshmeowllow cats will need their faces carefully piped using black marshmallow, so that they don't wash off in the hot chocolate!

5 / To assemble, first warm a plate in the microwave. Place the rim of one of the chocolate semispheres on the plate until just slightly melted (you can wear gloves if you want to avoid fingerprints on the chocolate, although this isn't necessary). Fill this semisphere with cocoa powder, sugar and a Marshmeowllow Cat, adding in any extra sprinkles/sweets, if you like too. Repeat the melting of the rim of the second semisphere, and press both together to seal in the filling. You can leave this as it is or pipe on or drizzle with some

melted white chocolate (make sure it isn't warm enough to melt the chocolate), then cover with sprinkles.

6 / To serve, place the bombe in a large mug half filled with hot milk, then pour on extra frothy milk, stir and watch as the chocolate melts and the marshmeowllow cat emerges!

CAT TIP "We will emerge covered in brown hot chocolate. Pour more hot milk on us to wash this away!"

Cat Got the Cream Canelé

Canelés and CATS! These cats have surely got the cream, by landing themselves right in the creamy custard-like interior of these canelés with their contrastingly dark, crisp and caramelized exterior.

It's best to make the batter for these in advance for the best flavour and texture, though I have made them the same day and they are still beautifully custard-like on the inside and crisp and golden on the outside. This batter is super simple and takes just 10 minutes to make.

For the most authentic result and irregular crumb structure, you would use copper moulds and a mixture of butter and beeswax to prevent sticking. However, these moulds are expensive and tricky to use, so I recommend using non-stick metal (steel or iron) moulds as they can be easily greased and you get a taller rise with a more regular crumb structure. They're just as delicious! You can also use silicone moulds, but they can result in slightly misshapen canelés, although they do still taste incredible.

Don't *fur*-get to make sure the oven is very hot and to bake these for as long as specified, so that the outside is dark brown and deeply caramelized.

DIFFICULTY 🐾 🐾 🐾

Can be made gluten-free
500ml [2 cups plus 2 Tbsp] whole milk
1 Tbsp vanilla bean paste (or 2 vanilla pods [beans])
200g [1 cup] caster or granulated sugar
2 medium eggs
2 egg yolks
50g [3½ Tbsp] salted butter, plus extra butter (or 60% beeswax and 40% butter), for greasing
100g [¾ cup] strong white bread flour (to make gluten-free, substitute with a gluten-free flour blend and ⅛ tsp xanthan gum)
3½ Tbsp rum (or substitute with citrus juice)

MAKES: 12–14 MEDIUM CANELÉS

ICING DRIP
60g [⅓ cup] icing [confectioners'] sugar
¾ tsp orange blossom water
1¼ tsp water
orange gel food dye

CREAM FILLING
300ml [¾ cup plus 2 Tbsp] double [heavy] cream
1½ tsp orange blossom water
orange and black gel food dyes
flaked [slivered] almonds

Note: Different brands of orange blossom water can have slightly different potencies, so it's always best to taste and check!

> **CAT TIPS** *"Leave the batter in the fridge for a few days and bake a small, fresh batch to treat yourself every day…*
>
> *You can play about using strawberries, and different sweets [candies] and cookies to make cute hats for us!"*

Continued overleaf

1 / Add the milk and vanilla to a small pan and heat until starting to simmer, then turn off the heat and leave to cool for about 3 minutes.

2 / Meanwhile, using a balloon whisk, whisk the sugar, eggs and egg yolks together in a large bowl. Melt the butter in the microwave for about 10 seconds, then whisk into the sugar and eggs until combined.

3 / Put the flour (plus xanthan gum, if gluten-free) into a separate bowl. Add a quarter of the milk mixture to the eggs and whisk in. Add a quarter of the flour and keep whisking. Keep alternating and mixing well, until everything is incorporated. Finally, add the rum (or citrus juice) and whisk again. Cover the bowl with plastic wrap, then chill in the fridge for at least 24 hours.

4 / When you're ready to bake, preheat the oven to 250°C [500°F/Gas mark 10] (or as high as your oven will go), then grease your metal moulds with a little softened butter.

5 / Fill the moulds with the batter, about 2cm [¾in] from the top, and bake for 10 minutes, then turn the oven down to 180°C [350°F/Gas mark 4] and bake for a further 45 minutes. The canelés should be a very deep, dark and caramelized brown colour on top.

6 / Remove from the moulds straight away, tapping if they are a little resistant to come out and place on a wire rack to cool.

7 / Once the canelés are cool, first slice off the top of each one and set aside, as these will be the lids.

8 / Next, make the icing [frosting] by whisking together the icing sugar, orange blossom water and water together in a bowl until smooth. Add enough orange food dye to colour. You may need to add a little extra icing sugar or water to adjust the consistency so that it isn't too thin or too thick – just test how it drips on the side of a cup until you're happy with the consistency. Spoon (or pipe) the icing onto the cut canelé, encouraging small drips down the sides.

9 / For the cream filling, whip the cream, orange blossom water and a little orange food dye together in a large bowl until soft peaks form. Be careful not to overwhip as it will end up getting overworked as you transfer it to the piping [pastry] bag and pipe. While whipping, gradually add very small amounts of food dye until an orange colour is achieved.

10 / Transfer about a quarter of the cream to a piping bag and cut a large tip or use a large round piping tip. Pipe a mound of cream on top of each canelé, refilling the piping bag when necessary. Place a small amount of the remaining cream in another small piping bag and cut a small tip or use a small piping tip. Use this to pipe on the paws.

Tip: Don't add all the cream at once to the piping bag as the cream at the top will become warm from your hands and it may also end up overwhipped by the time you get to pipe it out. You can fix slightly overwhipped cream by adding more liquid cream.

11 / Place a small piece of slivered almond for the nose/mouth area and insert small slivered almonds for the ears. You can use a small sharp knife to cut these so they are pointier and more cat-like.

12 / Place the reserved canelé lids back on top, then draw on facial details using a cocktail stick [toothpick] dipped into a very small amount of black food dye. Use a VERY minimal amount otherwise your cats will have big black and dripping eyes! These are best eaten the same day they are made. The black food dye will bleed into the cream once refrigerated, and the canelé exterior will become soft, so it's best to serve these immediately (not that you will be able to resist anyway).

Le Chat Parfait

Roasted balsamic strawberries, cream, ice cream, fresh strawberries, toasted almonds and chocolate… all topped with the cutest bundles of ice cream ever. What's not to like? The roasted balsamic strawberries sound unusual, but the balsamic vinegar adds an addictive depth of flavour and acidity which will make you never want to go back to ordinary strawberries. It's quick to do while also being an excellent way to use up any strawberries that aren't looking their best anymore.

You can also customize this recipe in many ways. Use your favourite ice cream, swap out the nuts for something else for that crunch, use different fruits, and create the cat face using sprinkles and whatever you happen to have in your cupboards.

DIFFICULTY 🐾 🐾
Unless it's a very hot day, in which case that can add an extra challenge!

MAKES: 4 LARGE PORTIONS

Can be made vegan and/or gluten-free

ROASTED BALSAMIC STRAWBERRIES
400g [14oz] strawberries, hulled and quartered
1 Tbsp balsamic vinegar
1 Tbsp caster or granulated sugar

TO ASSEMBLE THE PARFAITS
800g [1lb 12oz] favourite ice cream (ideally pale in colour so it contrasts with the strawberries and chocolate)
pink chocolate (candy melts or ruby chocolate) or pink sprinkles, for nose

wafer cone (chopped up), for ears (to make gluten-free, use gluten-free cones or use flaked [slivered] almonds for the cat ears)
edible eye sprinkles or black sesame seeds, for eyes
white edible wafer paper or long white sprinkles, for whiskers
200ml [scant 1 cup minus 2 Tbsp] double [heavy] cream (to make vegan, use your favourite whippable cream)
150g [5oz] dark [bittersweet] chocolate, finely chopped
4 Tbsp toasted flaked [slivered] almonds

Continued overleaf

> **CAT TIP** "Paw-ticularly if it's a hot day, we will melt very quickly at room temperature while you're decorating us! So have everything prepared, work close to the freezer, then decorate us one at a time. If it's a VERY hot day, then you could quickly decorate us while we're in the freezer."

1 / First, make the roasted balsamic strawberries. Preheat the oven to 180°C [350°F/Gas mark 4].

2 / Place the chopped strawberries in a shallow baking sheet and spoon over the vinegar and sugar. Toss to combine, then spread into a single layer and bake for around 30 minutes, stopping halfway to stir. The strawberries should have released a lot of their juices and shrunk down.

3 / Leave the strawberries to cool at room temperature, then chill in the fridge until completely cool.

4 / While the strawberries roast and chill, make the scoops of cat ice cream to top the parfait. Use an ice-cream scoop to create 8–12 round balls of ice cream (2–3 cats per parfait), then chill them in the freezer straight away.

5 / To decorate a cat ice-cream scoop, cut pink chocolate, candy melts or ruby chocolate into a nose shape, or you can use a sprinkle for the nose and press this into the middle of the ice-cream scoop. Cut cat ear shapes from a wafer cone and press these in for the ears. For the eyes, press on black sesame seeds or edible eye sprinkles. Insert white sprinkles for the whiskers, or you can use edible wafer paper cut to size (see photo), but this needs to be inserted just before eating otherwise it will go soggy! Repeat to decorate all the cat ice-cream scoops, and leave in the freezer until ready to serve.

6 / Return to the strawberries. Once they are cool, process

in a blender briefly until slightly smoother, but still with a little texture. Whip the cream in a bowl until soft peaks form. Place the finely chopped dark chocolate in a microwaveable bowl and microwave in 15–30-second bursts, stirring well after each burst until smooth and melted.

7 / Layer up your serving glasses, starting with the roasted strawberries, then add the whipped cream, some ice cream, toasted almonds and melted chocolate. Repeat until you fill the glass. Keep each glass in the freezer while you layer up the next.

8 / Carefully place 2–3 decorated cat scoops on top of each parfait to finish. Insert wafer paper whiskers if still needed, then serve straight away.

- SWEET TREATS -

Cheesecake to Whisker You Away

This is a baked New York-style cheesecake, and all the cool cats and kittens agree that it is creamy, smooth and pure de-*CAT*-ence. It also features a caramelized top, which you will love for its extra flavour and contrast.

The actual biscuit [cookie] base and cheesecake mixture takes very little time or effort to make – most of the time you will be relaxing while it bakes long and slow, then chilling to ensure pure cheesecake perfection. Bake this cheesecake the day before you want to serve it, then on the day simply remove it from the tin and sift over the cutest stencilled cat.

Wondering how to get a stencil? You can either buy one, or you can make it yourself in 15 minutes. Draw around the base of the cake tin onto a piece of plain and ordinary paper, then sketch a simple line drawing of a cat within the circle. Place the paper on a firm board or something that you don't mind getting scratched and use a sharp blade or knife to score the paper and cut it out. Be very careful not to cut your fingers! Remember that the icing sugar design will only transfer wherever the paper is removed (it's the negative image), so you need to cut on 2 sides of every line. Once you start, you will figure it out!

DIFFICULTY 🐾 🐾 🐾

This could even be 2 paws, because (beyond the usual disasters like forgetting it's in the oven and burning it) the worst that can happen is the cheesecake cracks or some water gets in, but there's not likely to be a big cat-astrophe and it'll still taste incredible.

SERVES: 12 (MAKES 1 X 23-CM [9-IN] CHEESECAKE)

Can be made vegan or gluten-free

BISCUIT BASE
340g [10½oz] digestive biscuits [graham crackers] or similar (you can also use your favourite gluten-free or vegan cookies, such as Biscoff cookies)
140g [½ cup plus 1 Tbsp] salted butter, melted, plus extra for greasing (or vegan butter – use one that's close to 80% fat content)

CHEESECAKE (SEE VEGAN ALTERNATIVE ON PAGE 105)
900g [4 cups] whole cream cheese, at room temperature
250g [1¼ cups] caster or granulated sugar
200g [¾ cup plus 1 Tbsp] sour cream
200ml [⅓ cup plus 1 Tbsp] double [heavy] cream
1 tsp salt
finely grated zest of 1 lemon
2 Tbsp lemon juice
1 Tbsp vanilla bean paste
2 medium eggs, room temperature
2 medium egg yolks, room temperature
2 Tbsp cornflour [cornstarch]

STENCIL DESIGN
2 Tbsp icing [confectioners'] sugar or cocoa powder (see page 105)

Continued overleaf

1 / Preheat the oven to 180°C [325°F/Gas mark 3]. Grease the base and sides of a 23-cm [9-in] springform tin (7cm [2¾in] high) with butter. Place a circle of baking paper (cut a little larger than the tin base) onto the base and clip on the side so that the paper is locked in, and a small amount of excess baking paper sticks out at the sides. This will help when removing the cheesecake from the tin later.

2 / For the biscuit base, use a food processor to blitz the digestive biscuits until fine, or place the biscuits in a large plastic bag and bash with a rolling pin or similar, until fine. Transfer to a large bowl, add the melted butter and mix until it resembles sand. Press into the base of the prepared tin, using the back of a tablespoon to help press and make sure it's as compact as possible.

3 / Bake for 10 minutes. Leave to cool, keeping the oven on.

4 / For the cheesecake, add the cream cheese and caster sugar to a large bowl and beat together until smooth, scraping down the sides of the bowl a couple of times. Be sure to mix at a slow speed and until just combined, to reduce the amount of air incorporated into the batter – as this can cause cracks. You can use a balloon whisk and mix by hand, or use a stand mixer fitted with the paddle attachment.

5 / Add the sour cream, double cream, salt, lemon zest and juice and vanilla and mix again at a slow speed until just combined.

6 / Add the eggs and yolks, one at a time, mixing slowly after each addition, and continuing to scrape down the bowl when necessary. Add the cornflour and whisk until combined again. The mixture will thicken slightly.

Tip: Make sure at all stages of mixing that you mix until the ingredients are just combined – you want to avoid incorporating air into the batter as this will cause cracking.

7 / Pour the mixture over the cooled biscuit base. It will be full almost to the brim – this is normal. Jiggle it side to side to smooth out the top of the cheesecake, then wrap the outsides of the tin with several layers of foil so that water from the water bath can't get in. Place the tin inside a larger tin or dish with raised sides that are at least three-quarters as tall as the cake tin. Place the cheesecake in the oven, along with the large tin or dish it's sat inside. Once it's in the oven, fill the outside tin with enough warm water to reach a quarter of the way up the sides of the springform tin. Make sure it doesn't go above the foil. (You could do this before putting it in the oven, but you risk getting water into the cheesecake when carrying it to the oven!)

Foil wrapping tip: Using foil that's on a longer roll will help ensure your cheesecake is properly watertight, as the water won't be able to get through the gaps where the foil overlaps.

8 / Bake for 30 minutes, then reduce the oven temperature to 150°C [300°F/Gas mark 2] and bake for a further 40 minutes, or until the cake is caramelized and brown on top, and not liquid but still jiggles as a whole (similar to jelly) when knocked. The edges should be puffed up but will sink down after cooling. After the baking time is up, turn the oven off but leave the cheesecake inside with the door closed for 30 minutes. Then open the oven door slightly and leave for a further 30 minutes.

Note: Don't open the oven door (particularly in the first half of baking time). Towards the end of the bake time, you can open the oven door to rotate the cheesecake, if necessary.

9 / Remove the cheesecake from the oven and water bath, then chill in the fridge for at least 5 hours, or ideally overnight.

10 / Once chilled, remove the cheesecake from the springform tin. The side should come off easily as the cheesecake naturally pulls away from the edges. Using the baking paper that's sticking out to help you, slide the cheesecake off the tin base and onto your serving plate, then slide the baking paper out from underneath.

11 / Place a stencil lightly on top (see the previous page), sift over the icing sugar and very carefully remove the stencil to reveal your design.

For the vegan alternative:

1.2kg [5⅓ cups] vegan whole cream cheese (around 23% fat content)
200g [¾ cup plus 1 Tbsp] vegan whole yogurt

300g [1½ cups] caster or granulated sugar
finely grated zest of 1 lemon
2 Tbsp lemon juice
1 tsp salt
1 Tbsp vanilla bean paste
50g [½ cup] cornflour [cornstarch]

CAT TIP You can slice up cheesecakes, both vegan and dairy-based, then cover in plastic wrap and freeze to make them last a lot longer! You can also enjoy eating the cheesecake from frozen too (like a cheesecake ice cream hybrid!).

1 / Preheat the oven to 180°C [325°F/Gas mark 3].

2 / Make the biscuit crust in the same way as the main recipe using the alternatives listed in the ingredients.

3 / For the cheesecake mixture, beat together all the ingredients in the same way, simply omitting the eggs and mixing for a little longer after adding the cornflour (it will become noticeably thicker after adding this).

4 / Bake in a water bath (see step 7) for 45 minutes, or until slightly golden and bubbling. This cheesecake won't brown as much as a dairy-based one: this is normal. It will also remain very liquid, but will firm up when chilled.

5 / Turn off the oven and leave the cheesecake in to cool for 1 hour, then refrigerate overnight.

6 / Unmould as normal, then decorate using cocoa powder for the stencilled cat face, as this will give greater contrast against the paler cheesecake compared to icing [confectioners'] sugar.

Pawfect Pancakes

Kittens leave pawprints all over your heart… and your pancakes. You will love these because there are just seven key ingredients and it takes only ten minutes to make the batter, then you simply cook them for the most pillowy and fluffy pancakes ever. Meowgnificent.

DIFFICULTY 🐾

Can be made gluten-free

3 medium eggs
80g [½ cup minus 1 Tbsp] caster or granulated sugar
⅓ tsp fine salt
50g [3½ Tbsp] butter, melted
1 tsp vanilla bean paste (optional but good)
300ml [1¼ cups] whole milk
270g [2 cups] plain [all-purpose] flour (to make gluten-free, substitute with a gluten-free plain

MAKES: AROUND 10

flour blend plus ¼ tsp xanthan gum)
3 tsp baking powder (or use gluten-free baking powder)

PLUS
butter or neutral-tasting oil, for frying the pancakes
unsweetened cocoa powder, for the pawprints
edible cats (see pages 12–23), optional

1 / Add the eggs, sugar, salt, melted butter and vanilla (if using) to a large bowl and beat together thoroughly until the sugar is dissolved.

2 / Add the milk along with the flour (plus xanthan gum, if gluten-free) and baking powder and mix until just combined – you don't want to overmix! You can sift the flour if it looks a little lumpy. The mixture should be thick but not as thick as cake batter. If it seems too thick, add a little extra milk until it's the correct consistency. At this point, you can add in any additional mix-ins such as berries or chocolate chips.

3 / Heat a frying pan [skillet] over a medium heat until it's

hot but not smoking. Smear the pan with a little butter or oil, then drop in a ladleful of batter. Cook for 2–3 minutes until the bubbles on the surface appear all over. Flip and cook on the other side until golden – this is a lot quicker than the other side so watch carefully. Transfer to a plate – you can keep this plate in the oven on a very low heat to keep warm.

4 / Repeat, using up all the batter to create a stack of pancakes.

5 / Place a pawprint stencil on top of a stack, then sift cocoa powder just over the stencil area. Carefully remove the stencil, decorate with an edible cat, if you like, and serve straight away.

CAT TIPS *For even MORE ameowzing pancakes, leave the batter in the fridge for a few hours or overnight, then cook them the next day. You can also add any mix-ins that you like to these. Try blueberries, raspberries, a little grated lemon zest, chocolate chips, etc.*

You can make a pawprint stencil yourself using card and a hole puncher. To make the larger/irregular-shaped hole, just punch through with the hole puncher, then cut with a pair of scissors to enlarge the hole and create the shape. This one is a bit fiddly to make though. If you don't have a stencil or don't have time to make one, just use a paintbrush and brush on cocoa powder into paw shapes.

Cosy Cats in Fruit Tarts

If tarts were cat sized, they would always have cosy cats in them. Well, actually... cats would try to sit in a tart, no matter how small it were. You won't be able to bear eating these cute kitty tarts, but the crisp and golden base, soft bed of pastry cream and sweet fruit will quickly change your mind.

DIFFICULTY 🐾 🐾 🐾 🐾

MAKES: 9 X 10-CM [4-IN] ROUND TARTLETS

Can be made vegan and/or gluten free

PASTRY
(or use store-bought pastry)
180g [1⅓ cups] plain [all-purpose] flour, plus extra for dusting (to make gluten-free, substitute with a gluten-free plain flour blend plus 1 tsp xanthan gum)
110g [½ cup minus ¼ Tbsp] slightly salted butter, cold, cubed, plus extra for greasing
30g [2½ Tbsp] caster or granulated sugar

2 Tbsp beaten egg (from 1 medium egg) (substitute with ice-cold water to make vegan, or substitute with aquafaba if making both vegan AND gluten-free as this will give the pastry more binding strength)

PASTRY CREAM (SEE VEGAN ALTERNATIVE ON PAGE 110)
6 medium egg yolks
135g [⅔ cup plus 1 tsp] caster or granulated sugar
30g [⅓ cup] cornflour [cornstarch]

450ml [2 cups minus 2 Tbsp] whole milk
1 Tbsp vanilla bean paste
15g [1 Tbsp] salted butter

PLUS
500g [1lb 2oz] favourite fresh berries and/or sliced fruit (I used raspberries, strawberries, blackberries and kiwis)
1 quantity 3D Cookie Cats (see page 12)
1 tsp apricot jam
a little warm water

1 / Grease 9 x 10-cm [4-in] loose-bottomed tartlet tins with butter.

Tip: You could also make this in one larger 22-cm [8½-in] tart tin with several cats nestled inside!

2 / Add the flour (plus xanthan gum, if gluten-free) to a large bowl. Add the cubed butter to the bowl, then rub the butter into the flour until it resembles fine breadcrumbs. Don't overwork. Stir in the caster sugar. Make a well, add the egg and beat with a fork, gradually combining it with the rest of the mixture. Use your hands to form the pastry into a ball. You can roll it out straight away, or wrap in plastic wrap

and leave to chill for 15 minutes, as this will make it easier to roll.

3 / Roll out the pastry on a well-floured surface and stamp out 9 circles to line each of the tart tins. Carefully lift and drape the pastry over the tins, then gently press the pastry into the edges of the tin and trim off the top edge. Prick the base a few times with a fork.

4 / Place the tart shells in the fridge for 20 minutes, or the freezer for 5–10 minutes. Meanwhile, preheat the oven to 180°C [350°F/Gas mark 4].

5 / When the tarts are chilled, cover with foil and fill with baking beans [pie weights]

(or rice or lentils), making sure they spread into all the edges. Blind bake for 10 minutes, then remove the foil and baking beans and bake for a further 10 minutes until the pastry is golden brown.

6 / Meanwhile, make the pastry cream (or see vegan alternative). Using a balloon whisk, whisk the egg yolks and sugar together in a large bowl until light and fluffy. Add the cornflour and whisk again until combined.

7 / Pour the milk into a large saucepan and heat over a medium heat until just before boiling. Add the vanilla, then immediately pour a quarter of the milk over the egg yolk mix,

Continued overleaf

whisking constantly as you do so. Whisk in the remaining milk, then pour the mixture back into the saucepan through a strainer and cook over a medium-high heat, whisking constantly, for 10–15 minutes until thickened. If it gets lumpy or thickens too quickly at any stage, remove the pan from the heat briefly and whisk rapidly. Once thickened, remove from the heat and stir in the butter.

8 / Transfer the pastry cream to a large bowl and leave to cool slightly, then cover with plastic wrap, making sure it touches the surface of the cream to prevent a skin forming. Chill in the fridge for at least 2 hours.

9 / When the tart shells are baked and golden brown, remove from the tart tins and leave to cool completely on a wire rack.

10 / When you are ready to serve, remove the pastry cream from the fridge and whisk it again until smooth (it can look lumpy after being chilled, but just needs a whisk). You can either spoon or pipe the pastry cream into your tart cases, then arrange the fruit on top and nestle a cosy cookie cat into each. To finish, brush the fruit with apricot jam watered down with a little warm water to give it a lovely shine. Store in an airtight container in the fridge for up to 2 days.

For the vegan alternative:

VEGAN PASTRY CREAM

450ml [2 cups] whole unsweetened plant-based milk

135g [⅔ cup plus 1 tsp] caster or granulated sugar

60g [½ cup plus 2 tsp] cornflour [cornstarch]

1 Tbsp vanilla bean paste

100g [½ cup minus 1 Tbsp] vegan butter (use one that's close to 80% fat content)

salt to taste, if the butter doesn't already contain this

1 / Whisk the milk, sugar, cornflour and vanilla together in a large saucepan until smooth, then whisk the mixture over a medium-high heat, making sure to prevent it from burning on the bottom of the pan. After around 5–10 minutes, the mixture should be smooth, thick and hold a trail. Remove from the heat and add the butter (and salt if needed). Chill and use in the same way as the dairy-based pastry cream.

"If I fits, I sits."

Sleeping Cats in Pain au Chocolat

Cats love to sleep in your bed, often mathematically calculating how to take over the whole bed despite their small size... so here they have been given their own comfy (and tasty!) pain au chocolat beds.

If you use store-bought puff pastry, the only actual 'baking' you will be doing is making the sleeping cookie cats! Even if you do make your own pastry this recipe is for rough puff rather than the much more labour intensive full puff, so it's quick and easy to make, but still gives you flaky buttery results.

DIFFICULTY ❁ to ❁ ❁

Can be made vegan or gluten-free

ROUGH PUFF PASTRY
150g [⅔ cup] salted butter, frozen in a block for at least 1 hour beforehand (or vegan butter – use one that's close to 80% fat content)
200g [1½ cups] plain [all-purpose] flour, plus extra for dusting (to make gluten-free, substitute with a gluten-free plain flour blend plus 1½ tsp xanthan gum)
2 Tbsp caster or granulated sugar
around 6 Tbsp ice-cold water

Or simply use 375g [13oz] store-bought, ready-rolled puff pastry and skip to step 2 of the method. Shop-bought pastry is often vegan, but do check the packaging. You can technically use vegan butter in this pastry recipe, but I'd recommend purchasing store-bought puff pastry for best results.

MAKES: 12

SLEEPING CATS
½ quantity of Calico Cats (page 117), omit the food dye and cocoa powder
plain [all-purpose] flour, for dusting (or use gluten-free substitute)
1 quantity Quick Black Icing (page 12)
(you will have some extra but that's a good thing! You could make cats that are trying to wake the ones in bed up!)

PLUS:
white, milk or dark chocolate squares, for the filling (about 2 squares, or about 15g [½oz] for each, so total 24 squares or 180g [6oz]) *Tip: You can also use biscoff spread!*
1 medium egg yolk, beaten (or 4 parts plant-based milk to 1 part liquid sugar, such as maple syrup), for brushing
icing [confectioners'] sugar, for sifting

Note: *This pastry recipe won't actually be as puffed as the store-bought, as it's only rough puff. But homemade full puff will take a lot longer, so this recipe has the best trade off of time/effort to end results.*

CAT TIP *"Try creating all sorts of different shaped versions of us (long, curled up, bendy...) and show our range of claw-ver ways of sleeping comfortably."*

Continued overleaf

1 / First, make the rough puff pastry. Working quickly, grate 100g [½ cup minus 1 Tbsp] of the frozen butter into the flour (plus xanthan gum, if gluten-free) using a standard cheese grater, add the sugar and stir. Gradually add enough water to form a dough (usually around 6 Tbsp). Wrap the dough in plastic wrap and chill in the freezer for 10 minutes. Place the remaining frozen butter back in the freezer too.

Tip: Keep the rest of the butter block in its wrapper and hold this end to avoid your warm paws melting the butter! As a general rule, try to work as fast as possible, and keep the butter as cold as possible!

2 / Once chilled, roll the dough out to a long rectangle, about 3 times as long as it's wide, and about 1cm [½in] thick. Grate the remaining frozen butter over the top two-thirds of dough, then fold the bottom third to the middle and the top third up and over that. You should now have a square shape with layers of butter and dough. Re-wrap in plastic wrap and chill in the fridge for 30 minutes.

3 / Once the pastry is chilled, line 1–2 baking sheets with baking paper. Roll out the rough puff pastry on a lightly floured surface to a rough rectangle, about 3mm (⅛ in) thick. Or simply unroll your store-bought puff pastry.

4 / Use a knife or pizza cutter to cut the dough into twelve 6 x 13-cm [2½ x 5-in] rectangles. Place each rectangle on the prepared baking sheet(s), spaced 3cm [1¼in] apart.

5 / Place chocolate squares or biscoff spread to cover the top half (leaving a 1cm [½in] gap at the top, and again in between the 2 chocolate squares), then place a cookie cat on top of the chocolate (imagining the chocolate is its pillow). Fold the bottom of the pastry up to cover the bottom of the cat, but leaving its head and arms exposed (like it's tucked up in bed). Use a fork to press and seal the edges together.

6 / Chill the baking sheets(s) for at least 30 minutes in the fridge, or 10 minutes in the freezer. Meanwhile, preheat the oven to 180°C [350°F/Gas Mark 4].

7 / Brush with beaten egg wash (or 4 parts plant-based milk to 1 part liquid sugar, such as maple syrup) and bake for 15–20 minutes (the homemade rough puff can take a little longer to bake).

8 / Leave to partially cool, then pipe sleepy cat faces using Quick Black Icing (see page 12) and dusting with icing sugar. Best eaten straight away!

TO MAKE THE SLEEPING CATS:

1 / Line a large baking sheet with baking paper. Make the dough following steps 2 and 3 on page 117. Roll the dough out on a floured work surface, then cut out 12 cat shapes that have little arms – either using a cutter or cutting around a homemade template. You will have remaining dough to make extra for snacking on! Transfer to the prepared baking sheet. then follow steps 7–8 on page 117 to bake and chill.

2 / Make the quick black icing following the instructions on page 12. Transfer the icing to a piping [pastry] bag, cut a small tip, ready to pipe the cat faces (see step 8, above).

"good meow-ning!"

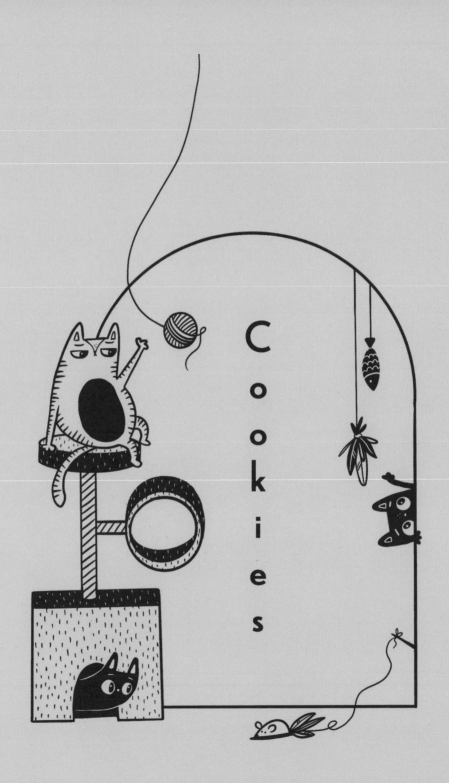

Cookies

Calico Cat Cookies

You don't need many ingredients or much time on your hands to create the most buttery and adorable shortbread kitties. And just like real calico kitties and their beautiful tri-colour fur, each one is unique and totally down to how you marble the dough and where YOU place the cutter!

DIFFICULTY ❀

MAKES: AROUND 30 SMALL CATS

Can be made vegan and/or gluten-free

200g [¾ cup plus 2 Tbsp] salted butter, at room temperature, cubed (or vegan butter – use one that's close to 80% fat content)

85g [½ cup minus 1 Tbsp] caster or granulated sugar
280g [2 cups plus 2 Tbsp] plain [all-purpose] flour, plus extra for dusting (to make gluten-free, substitute with a gluten-free plain flour blend plus ¾ tsp xanthan gum)

orange gel food dye
½ tsp unsweetened cocoa powder

1 / Line 2 baking sheets with baking paper or a silicone mat.

2 / Beat together the butter and sugar in a large bowl until smooth and spreadable.

3 / Add the flour (plus xanthan gum, if gluten-free) and mix until just combined. The dough should be slightly sticky, but soft and easy to handle.

4 / Pinch off 2 x 35-g [1¼-oz] pieces of dough and set aside the remaining larger piece. Mix orange food dye into one of the small pieces and cocoa powder into the other.

5 / If the dough feels too warm or soft, wrap it in plastic wrap and chill it in the fridge for 15–30 minutes until firm enough to roll out.

6 / Turn the dough out onto a well-floured surface and roll the large plain piece of dough out to around 5mm [¼in] thick. Press in pieces of the orange and brown dough all over randomly, then roll out again until around 4mm [⅛in] thick. Cut out cat shapes using cutters, then transfer to the prepared baking sheets. You will have some leftover dough, so press this together and roll

out again, being careful to prevent the colours from merging too much.

7 / Chill in the fridge for at least 30 minutes, or in the freezer for 10 minutes. Meanwhile, preheat the oven to 160°C [325°F/Gas mark 3].

8 / Bake for 10–12 minutes until just ever so lightly browned at the edges. Leave to cool for 10 minutes on the baking sheets, then carefully transfer to a wire rack to finish cooling. Store in an airtight container for 1–2 weeks.

"Did you know that we're known as the world's most colourful cats?"

Macaron Catarons

These are as *pawticular* as real cats, but so rewarding when you get it right. While this may be one of the trickier recipes in this book, I do have some tips and tricks for getting *pawsome* macarons:

- Make sure your almonds are ground up very finely.
- A non-stick silicone baking mat won't crease and cause your macarons to become misshapen (baking paper may do this if it creases). You can place any templates or guides underneath the silicone mat, as they are slightly see-through. You can also buy silicone mats with circle markings to guide you when piping.
- When piping, pipe from straight above rather than at an angle. This helps achieve a round and even shape.
- Don't skip banging the baking sheet on the work surface – this is important to get any large air bubbles out. If you don't, they may expand and cause the macaron surface to crack!
- Don't *fur*-get to give the macarons time to rest and form a skin!

Vegan tip: You can make these vegan by switching the egg white for chickpea water or aquafaba – and it's best if you can reduce down the aquafaba beforehand so the consistency is similar to egg whites. To reduce the aquafaba, just simmer over a medium-low heat for 30 minutes, or until it has reduced by about half, then leave to cool before using. You will also need to bake the vegan version at a lower temperature for longer as they are more sensitive to heat, but other than that, the same rules apply to both!

DIFFICULTY 🐾 🐾 🐾 🐾 🐾

MAKES: AROUND 20 MACARONS OR 2 BAKING SHEETS OF MACARONS (DOUBLE THE RECIPE FOR MORE)

CAT TIPS *"Pawlease don't let the sugar syrup go too hot otherwise it won't combine with the rest of the mixture!*

You can do lots of different colours once you get the hang of it! You can even pipe little tails, swirly macarons and eyes!"

Continued overleaf

Can be made vegan and naturally gluten-free

115g [½ cup plus 1¼ Tbsp] caster or granulated sugar
40ml [2⅔ Tbsp] water

MIXTURE A
105g [1 cup] finely ground and sifted almonds
105g [¾ cup plus 1½ Tbsp] sifted icing [confectioners'] sugar

40g [1½oz] egg white (or aquafaba [see tip on page 118])

MIXTURE B
45g [1½oz] egg white, at room temperature (or aquafaba [see tip on page 118])

CHOCOLATE GANACHE FILLING
250g [9oz] milk, semisweet or dark chocolate, finely chopped
200ml [1 cup minus 2 Tbsp] double [heavy] cream (to make vegan, use coconut milk)

PLUS
gel food dyes
black edible ink pen, or black gel food dye mixed with a tiny amount of water (to paint the face details after baking)

1 / First, line 2 baking sheets with baking paper or a silicone mat. Have any templates you will be using ready to hand and organized. Have all your piping [pastry] bags and any food dyes you will be using ready to hand.

2 / For Mixture A, stir the sifted ground almonds and icing sugar together in a large bowl. Add the egg white (or aquafaba) and mix until it forms a paste.

3 / Add Mixture B to a stand mixer (or use a handheld electric whisk) fitted with a balloon whisk attachment.

4 / Add the caster sugar and water to a pan and stir occasionally over a medium-high heat until the sugar has dissolved and the mixture starts to bubble. Start whisking the egg white (or aquafaba) to soft peaks. You want to time the sugar syrup reaching 115°C [239°F] with the egg white (or aquafaba) reaching soft peaks. You can always take the sugar syrup off the stove and/or slow the mixer (but don't turn it off) to time the two together.

Tip: The aquafaba will take longer to whisk to soft peaks than the egg white, so have this in mind when timing this with the sugar syrup reaching temperature.

5 / When the egg white (or aquafaba) has reached soft peaks and the sugar syrup is at 115°C [239°F], increase the speed of the mixer (or whisk) to high while pouring the sugar syrup in a thin stream down the side of the bowl (do not pour directly on the whisk).

6 / Once all the sugar has been poured in, continue whisking on high speed until the side of the bowl feels cool to the touch, 3–5 minutes or so. At this point, turn off the mixer and use a spatula to fold the meringue into Mixture A. Distribute the macaron mixture between bowls and add food dye to colour each individually, before transferring to piping bags.

7 / For cats without the two-tone colours, pipe round macarons onto the prepared baking sheets or mats, holding your piping bag (fitted with medium round piping tip, or simply cut a tip) in the centre of the circle and squeezing without moving the bag, then twizzling the tip to finish piping. The macarons should spread slightly after piping but still hold their shape, and the tip of the macarons should disappear within a minute or so.

8 / Next, you can pipe the ears. Just pipe these in place, trying to keep the mixture thick (similar to the rest of the face).

9 / After piping, pick up the baking sheet and bang it on a flat surface about 3 times. You should see air bubbles come to the surface. Some of them might pop of their own accord, but you might have to use a cocktail stick [toothpick] to help pop a few.

10 / Leave the macarons for around 30 minutes (or longer, see below) to form a slight skin, then add raised details on top (such as a nose, stripes, etc.) if you like.

Alternative: For cats with a two-tone face (or different coloured ears) you need to have a small/medium tip (or cut a tip on your piping bag) and use this to pipe the shape (as if you were piping icing on a cookie – except a lot thicker)

"Try decorating us as Maine coons, then you could say we are Maincaroons."

while leaving a space for the other colour. Immediately pipe on the other colour adjacent to it, completing the circular shape. Just make sure when you're using this method that you pipe the macarons as thick as you can. This is to ensure that their bubbly 'feet' still form when baking!

11 / Leave the macarons for another 1–2 hours to form a proper skin on the surface – you should be able to gently touch the macaron and it shouldn't come away on your finger. The time it takes for the macarons to form a skin depends on how humid the air is.

12 / When the macarons are ready, preheat the oven to 150°C [300°F/Gas mark 2] (or 120°C [250°F/Gas mark ½] for vegan macarons). Bake the egg white-based macarons for

15–18 minutes and the vegan macarons for 30 minutes. You know they are done when you tap them and they don't still move around on their 'feet'.

13 / Leave the macarons to cool, then peel off and add extra decorations using black edible ink pen or black food dye mixed with a tiny amount of water.

14 / Next, make the filling. Finely chop the chocolate and place in a heatproof bowl. Heat the double cream in a pan until *just* starting to bubble at the edges, then immediately pour over the chocolate. Leave for 2 minutes, then stir until all the chocolate has melted. If the chocolate hasn't melted, then give it a few 5–10-second bursts in the microwave, stirring well after each. Chill in the fridge for 15–30 minutes until it's no

longer warm to the touch, then whip for a few minutes until a little fluffier/thicker and paler in colour (the mixture should be similar in consistency to a soft buttercream). Transfer to a piping bag. If it gets too stiff, just microwave for 5 seconds. If it's too runny, leave it to chill for a little longer.

15 / Cut a medium tip in the piping bag (or use a round piping tip) and pipe the filling onto one half, then sandwich together.

16 / The macarons are best chilled in the fridge for a day or so before serving, as this helps to soften the shell – this is especially the case for the vegan macarons. Store in an airtight container in the fridge (separating each layer with a sheet of baking paper) for up to a week, or freeze for 3 months.

- COOKIES -

Ginger Snap Cats

These are exactly how grumpy ginger tom cats would be personified in cookie form. These little guys look fierce, but that fierceness belies a crisp and addictive cookie, with a little fiery ginger heat that warms your belly.

DIFFICULTY 🐾 🐾 It's only the decorating that nudges this up to 2 paws!

MAKES: 16

Can be made vegan and/or gluten-free

COOKIE DOUGH
150g [1 cup plus 2 Tbsp] self-raising flour (to make gluten-free, substitute with a gluten-free self-raising flour blend plus ¾ tsp xanthan gum)
1¼ tsp bicarbonate of soda [baking soda]
2½ tsp ground ginger
70g [⅓ cup plus 1 tsp] caster or granulated sugar

¼ tsp salt
75g [⅓ cup] unsalted butter, melted (or vegan butter – use one that's close to 80% fat content)
3 Tbsp golden [light corn] syrup

ROYAL ICING
½ quantity Royal Icing (page 127)
orange and black gel food dyes

Note: You only need to make ½ quantity of Royal Icing as it's hard to make a much smaller quantity and divide it up to create different colours. Any leftover icing can be piped out onto baking paper in long thin strands and left to dry. Once dry, chop up – and you have made sprinkles! Store these in an airtight jar and use to create more Sprinkles The Cat (page 127), or use to decorate other cats and kittens.

1 / Line 2 large baking sheets with baking paper.

2 / Add the flour (plus xanthan gum, if gluten-free), bicarbonate of soda, ginger, sugar and salt to a large bowl and stir until combined.

3 / Pour in the melted butter, add the golden syrup and stir until the mixture forms a soft dough.

4 / Roll the dough into a 25-cm [10-in] long log shape, then cut into 16 equal pieces. Roll each piece into a ball and place on the prepared baking sheets, spaced at least 5cm [2in] apart. Flatten each ball slightly with the back of a spoon –

they will spread during baking. Chill in the fridge for at least 30 minutes, or in the freezer for 10 minutes. Meanwhile, preheat the oven to 170°C [340°F/Gas mark 3].

5 / Bake for 12–15 minutes until cracked on top and deep golden in colour. Leave on the baking sheets for 10 minutes to firm up, then carefully transfer to a wire rack to finish cooling.

6 / While the biscuits cool, make the royal icing following the instructions on page 129. Leave a third of the icing white, then divide the remaining icing between 2 bowls. Dye one portion orange and the other black using gel food

dyes. Transfer the different icing colours to piping [pastry] bags, cutting a small tip in each. Pipe angry ginger tom cat faces onto each cookie and vary your designs so that each cat is quirky and unique. Store in an airtight container for 1–2 weeks.

CAT TIP *"Use a very small tip on your piping bags to give you control. You can also use a few sprinkles to enhance how we look. Don't be too quick to deem your piping a 'mistake' – as it could actually be the making of a hilariously angry cat, like me!"*

Black Cat Cookies

The cut-out cat silhouette is simple yet very effective, so you get to impress while not needing to do any detailed decorating! If you're in a rush, you could even make these using your favourite chocolate spread instead of ganache – making this a very speedy bake. The shortbread is incredibly buttery, and the kick of cinnamon, chocolate and orange will have you coming back for another cookie as soon as you finish one.

Make these for Halloween, or switch up the colours for any occasion. This recipe is inspired by my own black cat, Inki, with his eyes that glow against his dark fur.

DIFFICULTY ❀ to ❀ ❀

Can be made vegan and/or gluten-free

SHORTBREAD
230g [1 cup plus 1 tsp] salted butter, at room temperature, cubed (or vegan butter – use one that's close to 80% fat content)
110g [½ cup plus 1 Tbsp] caster or granulated sugar
finely grated zest of 1 orange
1½ tsp ground cinnamon
orange gel food dye
340g [2½ cups] plain [all-purpose] flour, plus extra for dusting (to make gluten-free, substitute with a gluten-free plain flour blend plus ¾ tsp xanthan gum)

MAKES: 12

GANACHE
190g [6¾oz] dark semisweet OR bittersweet chocolate
100ml [½ cup minus 2 tsp] double [heavy] cream (or use coconut milk to make vegan)
1½ Tbsp liquid glucose or golden [light corn] syrup (optional, but this will keep the ganache shiny)
black gel food dye

Tip: Or you can use your favourite chocolate spread instead of the ganache!

OPTIONAL
round sprinkles for eyes

Continued overleaf

1 / Line 2 baking sheets with baking paper or silicone mats.

2 / Add the butter and sugar to a large bowl and beat with a spoon or spatula until smooth. Add the orange zest and ground cinnamon and mix to combine. Mix in orange gel food dye to colour – aiming for a slightly brighter colour than the end result you're looking for, because it will be lighter after adding the flour and after baking.

3 / Add the flour (plus xanthan gum, if gluten-free) and use your hands to combine the dough into a ball. Avoid overworking/overmixing the dough at this point as the gluten in the flour will develop, which will make the final cookies tougher.

Tip: You can wrap the dough in plastic wrap and chill in the fridge for 30 minutes to make rolling out easier, particularly if it's a hot day.

4 / Roll out the dough on a lightly floured surface, then stamp out 24 round cookies using an 8-cm

[3¼-in] cookie cutter. Arrange on the prepared baking sheets, leaving at least 1cm [½in] between each, as they will spread slightly during baking. Use a cat-shaped cutter to stamp 12 of the circles, removing the cat-shaped centre. Leave to chill in the fridge for at least 30 minutes, or in the freezer for 10 minutes.

5 / Meanwhile, preheat the oven to 160°C [325°F/Gas mark 3].

6 / Bake the cookies for 10–15 minutes until just slightly starting to colour at the edges.

7 / Meanwhile, make the ganache. Finely chop the chocolate and place in a heatproof bowl. Heat the double cream in a pan until just starting to bubble at the edges (be careful not to make it too hot!), then immediately pour over the chocolate. Leave for 2 minutes, then stir until all the chocolate has melted. If the chocolate hasn't melted, then give it a few 5–10-second bursts in the microwave, stirring well after each.

8 / Stir in the liquid glucose (if using, but this will maintain a shiny finish to the ganache once it's set) and enough black food dye to make it look blacker. Leave to cool until thick enough to spread onto the cookies.

9 / When the cookies have finished baking, leave them on the baking sheets for 5 minutes, then carefully transfer them to a wire rack to finish cooling.

10 / Spoon the ganache in a circle on all the cookies that don't have the cut-out, using the back of a spoon to smooth it towards the edges, while also leaving a small border as the ganache will spread outwards when sandwiched. Sandwich with the cut-out cookies on top. You can leave the cookies like this or add extra sprinkles for eyes.

11 / Eat straight away or store in an airtight container for up to 2 days, or store in an airtight container in the fridge for a week.

Sprinkles The Cat

Sprinkles The Cat is truly committed to her love of sprinkles, both inside and out… Serve these to friends and they won't believe the sprinkle surprise after breaking these cuties in half!

Pssst. You can even write very tiny notes on edible paper (and it's useful here if you can write small!), and tuck one into each cookie pouch along with some sprinkles. Sort of like fortune cookies, except they're messages of happiness from Sprinkles The Cat.

DIFFICULTY 🐾 🐾 🐾

MAKES: AROUND 10–15 MEDIUM CATS

Can be made vegan and/or gluten free

200g [¾ cup plus 2 Tbsp] salted butter, at room temperature, cubed (or vegan butter – use one that's close to 80% fat content)
70g [⅓ cup plus 1 tsp] soft light brown sugar
2 tsp ground cinnamon
½ tsp ground ginger
⅛ tsp ground nutmeg
⅛ tsp ground white pepper
⅛ tsp ground cloves
pinch of bicarbonate of soda [baking soda]
280g [2 cups plus 2 Tbsp] plain [all-purpose] flour, plus extra for dusting (to make gluten-free, substitute with a gluten-free plain flour blend plus ¾ tsp xanthan gum)

ROYAL ICING

1 medium egg white (or 30–40g [1–1½oz] aquafaba or pasteurized egg white)
180–240g [1¼–1¾ cups] icing [confectioners'] sugar
black food dye

PLUS

sprinkles
1 x A4 sheet of edible wafer paper

> **CAT TIPS** *"Handle your dough like my grumpy brother! Touch it purposefully but gently, and only when necessary. Don't touch it if you don't need to. This is because the more you work the dough, the more the gluten will develop and result in tougher cookies. Likewise, the more you agitate a cat (or anyone!), the more upset it will feel.*
>
> *If you're not confident making your piping smooth and neat – embrace it. You can use a slightly stiffer icing and use a fork to create texture and my whiskers, then the sprinkles will enhance my cuteness!"*

Continued overleaf

1 / Line 2 baking sheets with baking paper.

2 / Add the butter and light brown sugar to a large bowl and beat together with a spoon or spatula until soft and smooth. Add all the spices and the bicarbonate of soda, then mix until combined.

3 / Add the flour (plus xanthan gum, if gluten-free) and mix until just combined. The dough should be slightly sticky, but soft and easy to handle.

Tip: When making cookies, beat the butter and sugar together until just combined and soft – it doesn't need to be light in colour and full of air, as you don't need the aeration and rise like you would do in cakes.

4 / Combine into a rough ball (wrap this in plastic wrap and chill in the fridge for 15 minutes or so, if it feels too soft to roll out), then roll out the dough on a floured work surface to the thickness of around 7.5mm–1cm [¼–½in].

5 / Cut out cat shapes using a medium cat-shaped cookie cutter, or by cutting around a homemade paper or cardboard template. Transfer the shapes to the prepared baking sheets, then use your finger to make as deep an indent as you can in the centre of the cookies, about 2–2.5cm [¾–1in] in diameter (or as big as you can make it!). Chill in the freezer for at least 10 minutes or in fridge for 30 minutes. Meanwhile, preheat the oven to 180°C [350°F/Gas mark 4].

6 / Bake for around 15 minutes, or until the edges are just starting to colour. While the cookies are still warm, press the indent in the cookie down again as it would have risen up a little during baking.

7 / Leave to cool on the baking sheets for 10 minutes, then carefully transfer to a wire rack to finish cooling.

8 / Meanwhile, make the royal icing. Whisk the egg white (or aquafaba) with 180g [1¼ cups] of the icing sugar together in a large bowl until smooth, then gradually keep adding icing sugar and whisking to combine until the consistency is thick enough to pipe. If you lift a spoon out and drizzle over the top, the trail should hold for about 15 seconds before disappearing. Place 1 Tbsp in a bowl and stir in black food dye to colour, then transfer to a piping [pastry] bag. Place 1 Tbsp of white icing in another bag and the remaining icing in a third bag. Cut a small tip in the 2 smaller piping bags and a medium tip in the other, or fit with round piping tips.

9 / When the cookies are cool, place as many sprinkles as you can in the indent while making sure these are flush with the surface of the cookie. Cut a small circle of edible wafer paper to fit over the top and cover the hidden sprinkles, sticking this down with icing and holding for a bit to make sure it stays stuck down. This will seal in the sprinkles, so that they will be revealed only when the cookie is broken in half. The edges of the wafer paper

might curl up a little after a while, but don't worry if it's just a little. However, if it's a lot then add a little more icing to stick it back down.

10 / Use the smaller piping bag filled with white icing to outline the whole cat shape, then 'flood' to fill in the entire outline using the piping bag with a bigger tip. You need to completely cover the cookies and the wafer paper which conceals the sprinkles. Scatter sprinkles all over the body of the cat, leaving a space for a face.

11 / Leave to semi-set for an hour or so (depending on humidity), then pipe the face details on top with the black icing. If you're not confident with piping the face, let the base white icing layer set for a few hours or overnight so it's completely hard, then any mistakes with the face can be wiped off and attempted again. Store in an airtight container for 2 weeks. The cookie will become soft from the icing, but will be delicious.

Pawsome Cookies

Cats are so relaxing when they purr, knead and make cookies with their paws. I imagine that these are the sorts of cookies they would make… Though theirs would probably contain fish for their own consumption… let's just pretend as if they'd make cookies humans would enjoy – extra short and buttery ones, with bursts of sweet jam that's baked in.

DIFFICULTY 🐾

Can be made vegan and/or gluten-free

200g [¾ cup plus 2 Tbsp] salted butter, at room temperature, cubed (or vegan butter – use one that's close to 80% fat content)
90g [½ cup minus 2 tsp] caster or granulated sugar
1 Tbsp vanilla bean paste

MAKES: 16

280g [2 cups plus 2 Tbsp] plain [all-purpose] flour (to make gluten-free, substitute with a gluten-free plain flour blend plus ¾ tsp xanthan gum)
100g [⅓ cup] your favourite jam

Tip: Use a variety of different jams for different flavours and colours.

1 / Line a rimmed baking sheet with baking paper or a silicone mat.

2 / Add the butter, sugar and vanilla to a large bowl and beat together with a spoon or spatula until smooth and spreadable.

3 / Add the flour (plus xanthan gum, if gluten-free) and mix until just combined. The dough should be slightly sticky, but soft and easy to handle.

4 / Divide the dough into 16 roughly equal pieces, then roll each piece into a rough ball and flatten with the palm of your hand.

5 / Arrange on the prepared baking sheet and press each cookie to create indents that resemble a cat paw – 1 larger indent with 4 smaller indents

around it. You can use your fingers, chopsticks or similar to create these indents.

6 / Chill in the fridge for 30 minutes, or in the freezer for 10 minutes, and preheat the oven to 160°C [325°F/Gas mark 3].

7 / Bake for 10 minutes, then remove from the oven and press the indents back down again (they will have risen up a little while baking). Using a small spoon, add a little jam to each indent, or put the jam into a piping [pastry] bag and pipe it into each indent, if easier. Return to the oven for another 10 minutes, or until just ever so lightly browned at the edges and the jam looks set. Leave to cool on the baking sheet for 10 minutes, then carefully transfer to a wire rack to finish cooling. Store in an airtight container for 1–2 weeks.

"I can make cookies too!"

- COOKIES -

Miso Tasty Cookie Cats

Not only are these easy to make and taste amazing (all thanks to the earthy, slightly nutty secret ingredient that is miso!), there's also a simple joy to be had from raiding the kitchen drawers to see the different sized forks in your cutlery drawer and various sprinkles to find out what kind of whiskers they can create!

DIFFICULTY ❀

MAKES: 16

Can be made vegan and/or gluten free

COOKIE DOUGH

100g [7oz] unsalted butter, at room temperature, cubed (or vegan butter – use one that's close to 80% fat content)

70g [⅓ cup plus 1 tsp] caster or granulated sugar

1 Tbsp white miso paste (reducé the amount if you're using other types of miso as they may be saltier and stronger)

150g [⅔ cup] plain flour (to make gluten-free, substitute with a gluten-free plain flour blend plus ½ tsp xanthan gum)

TO DECORATE

bake-stable sprinkles (do a test cookie with your sprinkles, as some sprinkles are bake stable and others will melt!)

edible eye sprinkles (or use various nuts and seeds to create eyes – see what you have in your cupboards)

colourful chocolate or chocolate chips (optional)

1 / Preheat the oven to 160°C [325°F/Gas mark 3] and line 1–2 baking sheets with baking paper.

2 / Add the butter and sugar to a large bowl and beat together with a spoon or spatula until smooth. Add the miso paste and mix in. Add the flour (plus xanthan gum, if gluten-free) and mix in with a spoon or spatula, then use your hands to form a dough.

3 / Roll the dough into a 22-cm [8½-in] long log, then pinch the log down its whole length and on both sides, so that it has pointed ears all the way down. Wrap loosely in plastic wrap and chill in the fridge for at least 30 minutes, or in the freezer for 10 minutes.

4 / Cut the chilled log into 16 slices and place on the prepared baking sheets, spaced well apart. Create whiskers using sprinkles (make sure they are bake stable), or with fork imprints. To create a fork imprint, dip a fork into a small bowl of water and use to flatten the sides of each cookie, pressing down to about halfway to resemble whiskers. Add flaked almonds, pumpkin seeds and/or sprinkles (there's lots of different options) for the eyes, then add a sprinkle (or more nuts or chocolate) for the nose. Just vary all the different faces with random bits and pieces from your cupboards to create a quirky bunch of cats. Once all are decorated, chill the shortbread again for at least 20 minutes in the fridge, or 5 minutes in the freezer.

5 / Bake for 10–12 minutes until pale and golden at the edges. Transfer to a wire rack to cool completely. Store in an airtight container for 1–2 weeks.

CAT TIP *"To give me a marbled look, tear off pieces from the main dough and knead in food dye. Then combine the different coloured doughs into one and continue from step 3. When you slice into the log, you'll get a whole family of us with different patterned coats! Add any non-bake ingredients (such as my eyes) after baking and cooling, using icing to stick."*

Schrödinger's Cat Box

Named after the quantum mechanic thought experiment… except that this is practical, tasty and brings a smile to anyone you gift it to.

This is a recipe for an edible cookie box which will display all your cat cookie creations made from the recipes in the rest of this chapter. And you can make as many or as few different types of cookies as you like!

For the templates: You will need to cut the following shapes from paper or card: 2 x A4 rectangles (one for the base and one for the lid (although a lid is optional!), two 30 x 7cm [12 x 2¾in] pieces (for the 2 longer sides), and two 20.5 x 7cm [8 x 2¾in] pieces (for the 2 shorter sides).

Make a lid for your box, and paw-sonalize it by piping the lucky recipient's name in royal icing!

DIFFICULTY 🐾 🐾 🐾 or, if making more cookies, 🐾 🐾 🐾 🐾 🐾
(Depending on how many different cookies you're putting in, this one isn't difficult but will take a little time to put together!)

MAKES: 1 LARGE SHARING-SIZE BOX OF COOKIES

Can be made vegan and/or gluten free

250g [1 cup plus 2 Tbsp] salted butter, at room temperature, cubed (or vegan butter – use one that's close to 80% fat content)
240g [1¼ cups] dark muscovado [soft brown] sugar
4 tsp black treacle [molasses]
4 Tbsp ground ginger
1½ Tbsp ground cinnamon
½ tsp ground cloves
4 Tbsp beaten egg (or use aquafaba)
¼ tsp salt

450g [3½ cups] plain [all-purpose] flour, plus extra for dusting (to make gluten-free, substitute with a gluten-free plain flour blend plus 1¼ tsp xanthan gum)

HARD CARAMEL
200g [1 cup] caster or granulated sugar
3 Tbsp water

ROYAL ICING (OPTIONAL)
see page 127
gel food dyes

"What if my human isn't my pet… but I'm the pet…?"

Continued overleaf

1 / Add the butter, muscovado sugar, salt and black treacle to a large bowl and beat together with a spoon or flexible spatula until smooth and soft.

2 / Add the ginger, cinnamon, cloves and beaten egg, and mix until just combined. Add the flour (plus xanthan gum, if gluten-free) and, using your hands, combine the dough until it forms a ball. If you feel like the dough is a little soft, wrap it in plastic wrap and refrigerate for 15 minutes, or so.

3 / Place half the dough on a piece of baking paper (that can fit on the baking sheet you will be using), scatter flour on top to prevent sticking, then roll out the dough, about 3mm (⅛ in) thick. Place paper or card templates on top and cut around to create panel shapes. Remove the excess dough surrounding the shapes and slide the baking paper onto a baking sheet. Repeat this process using the second half of dough with a second sheet of baking paper/another baking sheet, to make the remaining templated shapes required (see template note on page 134). You may need a third baking sheet depending on their sizes. Reroll any dough when necessary.

Tip: Rolling the dough directly onto the baking paper means it won't become misshapen when having to transfer it from the work surface to the baking sheet.

4 / Chill the dough in the fridge for at least 30 minutes, or 10 minutes in the freezer. Meanwhile, preheat the oven to 170°C [340°F/Gas mark 3].

5 / Bake the cookies for 12–20 minutes until just beginning to colour. Larger pieces will need longer to bake. If any of the edges aren't quite straight after baking, you can cut them with a knife while the dough is still warm. Leave to cool on the baking sheet for 10 minutes, then carefully transfer them to a wire rack to finish cooling.

6 / Meanwhile, make the royal icing following the instructions on page 129. Colour as desired using food dyes, then transfer to piping [pastry] bags. Use the icing to pipe your own designs on the individual panels (they are easier to pipe onto before assembling the box). You can customize this box for a gift and write the lucky recipients' names on the lid!

7 / Once the designs are piped on, make the caramel. Add the sugar and water to a large saucepan (ideally one large enough so that the longest side of the cookie can be dipped into it) and stir briefly just so the sugar is mixed with the water. Heat over a high heat until a deep golden colour. Keep an eye on the pan as the sugar starts to bubble and darken. You can also swirl the pan ever so slightly once the caramel starts to take on some colour, but don't stir as this can cause it to crystallize and become grainy.

8 / Once the caramel is the desired colour, dip the cookie sides (starting with one of the longest sides) into the caramel and use this to assemble the box. Once you attach a side with the caramel, hold it for 30 seconds, or until it feels set. You can also prop it up with various household objects.

9 / Once the box is assembled, arrange your selection of cookies inside – whether you want to have all of these homemade, none of these homemade, or homemade with a mixture of store-bought cookies! You can use bits of string to tie up some cookies to make it extra pretty. If you made a lid, loosely place it on top and your Schrödinger's cat box is complete.

Langue de Chat

These classic French cookies *litter*-ally translate to 'cat tongues' because their elongated shape resembles a cat tongue. But cat tongues wouldn't be so cute, right? So I've designed these as super cute paws. I suppose you could call them *patte de chat* instead...

These are *purr*-suasive when served with a steaming cup of tea or coffee, and you will love the crisp edges and slightly chewy centre.

The vegan version is snappier/won't have the slight chew in the middle, but they are just as tasty – just uniquely different!

DIFFICULTY
These are actually mind-blowingly simple to make and the batter itself takes just 5 minutes to mix up. The difficulty is only higher because of the piping and the decorating.

MAKES: 30

Can be made vegan and/or gluten free

COOKIE BATTER
125g [½ cup plus 1 Tbsp] salted butter, room temperature, cubed (or vegan butter – use one that's close to 80% fat content)
125g [¾ cup plus 2 Tbsp] icing [confectioners'] sugar
1 tsp vanilla bean paste
3–4 egg whites (should total about 125g [4oz]) (or use aquafaba)
160g [1¼ cups] plain [all-purpose] flour (to make gluten-free, substitute with a gluten-free plain flour blend but without xanthan gum)

TO DECORATE
100g [3½oz] milk or dark (or a mixture) chocolate, roughly chopped
100g [3½oz] white chocolate, roughly chopped (you can also buy vegan chocolate to use)
pink food dye for chocolate (make sure it's oil based – if it contains water then it will make the chocolate seize)

Continued overleaf

1 / Line 2 baking sheets with baking paper or a silicone mat. Preheat the oven to 180°C [350°F/Gas mark 4].

2 / Add the cubed butter to a large bowl, along with the icing sugar and vanilla. Beat with a spoon or flexible spatula until smooth and combined.

Tip: The butter being at room temperature is key to this recipe as the batter should be easy to pipe (similar to buttercream consistency). If it's a hot day and the batter is runny, then pop the piping [pastry] bag into the fridge to chill for a bit.

3 / Add the egg whites, one at a time, whisking after each addition. The butter will look split and not be fully incorporated, but that's normal at this stage.

4 / Add the flour and mix until just combined.

5 / Transfer the batter to a piping [pastry] bag, then cut a 1-cm [½-in] tip (or fit the bag with a 1-cm [½-in] round piping tip). Pipe thin straight lines that are about 8cm [3¼in] long, onto the prepared baking sheets, leaving about 5cm [2in] between each one, as they will spread during baking.

6 / Bake for 10 minutes until golden brown around the edges. Use a palette knife to transfer the cookies to a wire rack to finish cooling.

7 / While they cool, melt the different types of chocolate in separate bowls in the microwave. Use 10–15-second bursts, stirring well after each.

8 / When the cookies are cool, dip them into the melted chocolate, then place them on a wire rack so the excess chocolate can drip off. Freeze for 5 minutes, or until set.

9 / At this point, if the bowls of chocolate are looking a little set, then microwave them in the same way as before again. Put 1 Tbsp of the white chocolate into a piping bag, and the milk and/or dark chocolate into separate piping bags. Stir in an oil-based pink food dye to colour the remaining white chocolate in the bowl, then also transfer this to a piping bag. Cut a small tip on all, and use the pink chocolate to pipe the pink paw details, and the other chocolate to pipe stripes and cat markings. Chill in the freezer for 2 minutes to set. These are best eaten immediately on the same day, but you can store them in an airtight container for 2 days – they will just lose their crispness at the edges.

"Our paws come in all shapes and sizes but they're all worthy of love, so don't worry if these come out of the oven all a little different! That's what makes them charming."

Breads

Sticky Kitty Buns

Usually, cats don't like sticky things on their paws, but there's always those quirky, lovable, weird cats who can't resist for some reason.

CAT TIP Use metal or silicone muffin tin(s) with large, deep holes. If using smaller cupcake tins, then divide the caramel topping between more holes, and cut the dough into smaller portions accordingly in step 7.

You will join these cats in LOVING these extremely soft and fluffy yet caramelized buns. The caramel is baked with the buns (kind of like an upside-down cake), so it's extremely satisfying when you flip your tin over and watch as the caramel and caramelized nuts are unveiled and drip down. Then there's another moment of satisfaction when you slice the buns open and see the spirals of dough inside, packed with even more flavour.

You can always omit the nuts, if you like.

DIFFICULTY 🐾 🐾 🐾

MAKES: 15 LARGE BUNS; IF YOU'RE USING A SMALLER TIN FOR THESE, YOU MAY NEED TO SLICE THE DOUGH INTO SMALLER PORTIONS AND MAKE MORE THAN 15

Can be made vegan

TANGZHONG PASTE
100ml [⅓ cup plus 1 Tbsp] water
25g [2¾ tsp] strong white flour

DOUGH
160ml [¾ cup minus 1 Tbsp] whole milk (or use plant-based milk)
80g [⅓ cup] salted butter (or vegan butter – use one that's close to 80% fat content)
neutral-tasting oil, for oiling
1 large egg (or replace with 30ml [2 Tbsp] vegetable oil and 30ml [2 Tbsp] plant-based milk)
finely grated zest of 1 orange
50g [¼ cup] caster or granulated sugar
1 tsp salt
420g [3 cups] strong white bread flour, plus extra for dusting
7g [2¼ tsp] instant fast-action yeast

FILLING
2 tsp ground cinnamon
100g [½ cup] light muscovado [soft brown] sugar
130g [1 cup plus 1 Tbsp] pecan nuts
80g [⅓ cup] salted butter, melted, for brushing (or vegan butter – use one that's close to 80% fat content)

CARAMEL TOPPING
115g [½ cup] salted butter (or vegan butter – use one that's close to 80% fat content)
135g light muscovado [soft brown] sugar
45ml [3 Tbsp] whole milk (or use plant-based milk)
80ml [⅓ cup] maple syrup
200g [2 cups minus 2 tsp] chopped pecans

TO DECORATE
cat decoration (page 145)

Continued overleaf

1 / First, make the *tangzhong* paste. Using a balloon whisk, mix the water and flour together in a pan until smooth. Place the pan over a medium heat and stir constantly with a spatula until the mixture has thickened to a pudding-like consistency. Pour into a bowl, cover with plastic wrap (making sure it touches the surface of the *tangzhong*) and chill in the freezer for 10 minutes.

2 / Meanwhile, for the dough, warm the milk in the microwave – it should be warm, not hot – then melt the butter in the microwave. Lightly oil a large bowl.

3 / Place the milk, butter, egg, orange zest, caster sugar, salt and chilled *tangzhong* in another large bowl and whisk briefly, then add the flour and yeast on top. To knead by hand, use a spoon to mix the wet and dry ingredients together until it forms a rough shaggy ball of dough, then turn out onto a floured surface and knead by hand until the dough is smooth and elastic. The dough will be sticky to start with, but avoid adding extra flour as much as possible – it will gradually become less sticky. Use a little oil to prevent it sticking. A dough scraper also helps to remove any dough that sticks to the work surface. Alternatively, use a stand mixer or bread machine fitted with the dough hook attachment to knead the dough for 10 minutes.

4 / Place the dough in the lightly oiled bowl and cover with lightly oiled plastic wrap, then leave to rise at room temperature until doubled in size.

5 / Meanwhile, make the filling. Place all the ingredients, except the butter, into a food processor and blend until fine but still with some texture and chunkier pieces. If you don't have a food processor, just roughly chop the nuts and mix with the sugar and cinnamon. Set aside.

6 / Next, make the caramel topping for the buns. Place the butter, muscovado sugar, milk and maple syrup into a pan and stir over a medium heat until the sugar and butter have melted. Leave to simmer for 1 minute. Divide the roughly chopped pecans evenly between each muffin hole then add 2 Tbsp of caramel to each.

7 / Once the dough has risen, the buns are ready to shape. Place the dough on a floured or oiled surface, then roll out to a 50 x 25-cm [20 x 10-in] rectangle. You will find that the dough keeps trying to shrink back due to the gluten development. If you're struggling to roll it out, just leave it for a few minutes to allow the gluten to relax, then return and roll it out further. Cover the surface of the dough with the melted butter, followed by the blitzed filling, then roll up the dough starting from the longer edge, into a sausage shape. Use a sharp knife and a sawing motion to cut this into 15 equal-sized pieces.

8 / Place a spiral of dough in each muffin hole on top of the pecans and caramel. Cover with lightly oiled plastic wrap and leave to prove at room temperature until doubled in size. Preheat the oven to 180°C [350°F/Gas mark 4] just before they are ready to bake.

9 / Bake for 15–20 minutes, or until golden on top.

10 / Once the buns are baked, leave them to cool for 2 minutes, then flip the whole tray over onto a wire rack, letting the caramel drip down. You may want to put a sheet of baking paper underneath the wire rack to catch any drips. Leave to cool, then insert the cats on top and enjoy! Store in an airtight container for up to 5 days. A quick blast in the microwave will soften them again.

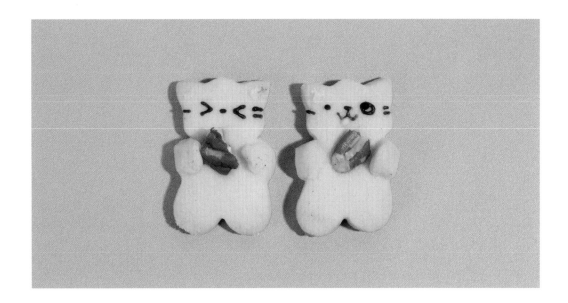

To make the cat decoration:

This recipe makes more dough than you'll need. You can make more cats or simply snack on the extra dough!

SHORTBREAD CATS
½ quantity of Calico Cats
   (page 117); omit food dye or
   unsweetened cocoa powder
plain [all-purpose] flour, for dusting
around 5 pecans, broken into thirds

QUICK BLACK ICING
1 quantity (see page 12)

1 / Line a large baking sheet with baking paper. Make the cats following steps 2 and 3 on page 117. Roll the dough out on a floured work surface, then cut out cat shapes that have little arms – either using a cutter or cutting around a homemade template. You will need 15 to decorate the buns, but the remaining dough can be used to make extra! Transfer to the prepared baking sheet. Place a small piece of pecan in between the arms of each cat, then fold the arms over so it looks like the cat is holding the nut. The dough may crack as you fold the arm over, so just press it until the crack is sealed again. Then follow steps 7–8 on page 117.

2 / Make the quick black icing following the instructions on page 14. Transfer the icing to a piping [pastry] bag, cut a small tip and use this to pipe the cat faces. You can also use pink icing for your kitties' ears and tongues, if you like.

Soup with a Dif-*fur*-ence

How to make soup MUCH more fun and cute? Float soft and fluffy cat bread in it, and add some fish-shaped croutons for the cat to play with. If you've never made your own croutons before, you're in for a real treat; you will never go back!

Use your favourite soup to serve these in!

DIFFICULTY 🐾 🐾 🐾

MAKES: ENOUGH FOR ROUGHLY 12 CAT BREADS (DEPENDING ON SIZE)
This will most likely be too many to serve in soup, but just bake the extras as cute cats.

Can be made vegan

Tangzhong bread dough (see page 143)

FISH CROUTONS
a few slices of bread (any bread will work but simple white soft sandwich bread is one of the easiest to cut into shapes)

salted butter, melted (or use vegan butter)
salt and freshly ground black pepper
dried Italian herbs, for sprinkling (optional)

PLUS
1 medium egg yolk, beaten (or 4 parts plant-based milk to 1 part liquid syrup, such as maple syrup)

black edible ink pen or black food dye mixed with a tiny amount of water
pink edible ink pen or pink food dye mixed with a small amount of water
your favourite soup

1 / Line a large baking sheet with baking paper. Follow the instructions for making the bread on page 144, then after the first rise, shape the dough so that you're creating a cat head and 4 separate paws. See step 6 on page 169 for instructions on the cat head shaping. For the paws, simply shape a small round ball, then repeat to make as many portions as you need. There will most likely be more than enough dough to make cats for the number of soup bowls you're looking to serve, so shape the remaining dough into a complete cat (with body, paws and tails), pressing firmly to make sure all the dough sticks together. This will serve as extra cat bread to dip in soup!

2 / Place on the prepared baking sheet (spaced out to allow each to rise), then cover loosely with oiled plastic wrap and leave to rise again until doubled in size.

3 / Preheat the oven to 180°C [350°F/Gas mark 4], then brush with beaten egg (or 4 parts plant-based milk to 1 part liquid syrup, such as maple syrup) and bake for 15 minutes, or until lightly browned. Leave to cool.

4 / Once cool, use a black edible ink pen or black food dye mixed with a little water and a paintbrush to paint on the facial details. You can also add a tongue using pink food dye mixed with a small amount of water or a pink edible ink pen.

5 / To make the croutons, preheat the oven to 180°C [350°F/Gas mark 4] and line a large baking sheet with baking paper. Cut your bread, using a knife or scissors, into simple fish shapes.

6 / Arrange the croutons in a single layer on the prepared sheet. Brush both sides with melted butter and season with salt and pepper. You can also sprinkle on Italian seasoning, if you like. Bake for 10–15 minutes until deep golden. The baking time depends on the size of your croutons.

7 / Arrange the floating cat bread in your chosen soup and place the fish croutons all around. Serve.

Meow, Bao!

I've made sleek black cats (or mini panthers!) here, but you can dye the dough to match your own cats. These are simply filled with chocolates, so they're very quick and easy, and when these are warm from the steamer, you will love watching the chocolate generously oozing out.

If you haven't steamed buns before, you need a saucepan filled with water, and a bamboo steamer and lid that will fit neatly on top. Don't try to bake these in the oven – the steaming is what makes these so soft, fluffy and irresistible.

DIFFICULTY 🐾 🐾 🐾 🐾

I've given this a higher difficulty mostly because of the shaping of the bao and the steaming method – in case steaming is something you're not used to doing frequently. But this really isn't that difficult if you've steamed dough before!

MAKES: 12

Can be made vegan

BAO DOUGH

300g [2¼ cups] plain [all-purpose] flour, plus extra for dusting
3g [½ tsp] instant fast-action dried yeast
3g [½ tsp] salt
60g [5 Tbsp] caster or granulated sugar
90ml [6 Tbsp] milk (or any plant-based milk)
80ml [⅓ cup] water
1 Tbsp vegetable oil, plus extra for oiling
green, pink and black gel food dyes

FILLING

12 chocolates (use ones with different fillings – from caramel to fruit flavours – to give endless different surprises in each bao)

CAT TIP *You can leave these plain (simply omit the sugar and chocolate) to serve alongside a meal, or add any filling you like, not just chocolate. You could even add a savoury filling! Just make sure that any filling you add is on the firmer side and not liquid-y – otherwise shaping will prove a little tricky! Some filling ideas are: red bean paste, black bean paste, firm custard, char siu (or veggie versions).*

"check meowt!"

Continued overleaf

1 / If using a stand mixer, add all the dough ingredients (except the food dyes) to a stand mixer bowl fitted with a dough hook attachment, ensuring the yeast doesn't directly touch the salt. Let the machine knead the mixture for about 8 minutes, or until the dough is smooth and elastic.

Tip: If kneading by hand, add the flour, yeast, salt and sugar to a large bowl and stir together. Add the milk, water and vegetable oil, stir together, then use your hands to combine into a rough ball of dough. Turn the dough out onto a lightly floured or oiled surface, and knead until the dough is elastic and smooth.

2 / Tear off a small pinch of dough, about the size of a large marble, and set aside (leave this uncoloured). Pinch off another similar-sized piece of dough and knead green food dye into it to colour. Pinch off a third similar-sized piece, this time kneading in pink food dye.

3 / Knead black food dye into the remaining larger piece of dough. This is a large quantity of dough to knead the dye into, so it will take a little time and patience by hand. It helps if you are lucky enough to have a mixer. You will also need to be quite generous with the black food dye, but do give it time to make sure all the colour is distributed evenly throughout the dough. The dough will become a little sticky if working by hand, so use a little extra flour to help, but avoid adding it as much as possible.

4 / You should now have a large ball of black dough and marble-sized pieces of white, pink and green dough. Place the dough in a lightly oiled bowl (separating the different colours with a little plastic wrap), then cover the bowl with lightly oiled plastic wrap. Leave to rise at room temperature for about 1 hour, or until it has doubled in size.

5 / When the dough has risen, remove 2 Tbsp of the black dough and set aside. Divide the remaining black dough into 12 equal pieces. They will be a bit sticky, so be sure to coat your hands and the dough with flour when handling. To shape the bao, use your fingers to stretch the dough into a small circle, which is thinner at the edges than in the centre, then add a chocolate to the centre.

6 / Gather the edges up and press together very firmly to seal in the filling. Turn the bun smooth side up. Try to make sure the surface is as smooth and taut as possible. Place on a small square of baking paper. You can also place some in the bamboo steamer at this stage, if you like. Just make sure they are generously spaced out as they will almost double in size when steamed.

7 / Use the reserved piece of black dough to create little ears for each bun, pressing firmly to make sure they adhere and won't fall off when steamed. Shape the eyes using the green dough, use a little white dough for the pupils, and use pink dough for the nose. Use the tiniest dab of water to help all of them stick to the smooth black surface. Try to exaggerate the facial features in size, slightly – as the final steamed bun will be doubled in size and the face details don't expand in size quite as much.

8 / Cover the bao (making sure they are well spaced out) with lightly oiled plastic wrap and leave to prove for around 30 minutes (though this varies depending on the room temperature) until they are about 50% bigger than before (not doubled in size).

9 / When risen, set the bamboo steamer over a saucepan of simmering water and steam the first batch of buns for 10 minutes over a low heat. Turn off the heat and leave in the steamer for 5 minutes before removing the lid. Remove the buns, refill the bamboo steamer with more bao and steam again. Serve straight away to enjoy the oozing chocolate!

Tip: After several hours, the bao will become hard and dry looking, but once you reheat them they go back to being soft and fluffy. Ideally, steam them again, or if in a pinch, heat in the microwave for 15 seconds or so.

Fat Cat Pizza!

The cutest and chonkiest fat cat in its spiritual food form: PIZZA! Get all your friends and family involved in decorating their own with their favourite toppings, then just enjoy the beauty of wholesome homemade (CAT!) pizzas!

DIFFICULTY 🐾 🐾

Can be made vegan

DOUGH

400g [2¾ cups] strong white flour, plus extra for dusting
2 tsp salt
7g [2¼ tsp] instant fast-action dried yeast
280ml [1¼ cups minus 4 tsp] water (use tepid water to speed up the rise if you're in a rush, but this isn't necessary)
20ml [4 tsp] olive oil, plus extra for oiling

TOPPINGS

around 10 Tbsp (150g) tomato sauce for pizza (see below)
1 Tbsp capers

MAKES: 3 SMALL PIZZAS

200g [7oz] mozzarella (drained weight) (or use vegan mozzarella)
a couple of black olives, for the cat face
black gel food dye mixed with a tiny amount of water, for painting cat whiskers
handful of fresh basil
salt and freshly ground black pepper
extra olive oil, for drizzling

OR
use any toppings of your choice

PLUS
semolina flour for underneath the pizza (optional but gives extra crunch)

To make the tomato sauce:

(Makes more than you need, but you can use this for all sorts!):
2 Tbsp olive oil
2 cloves of garlic, finely chopped
2 Tbsp concentrated tomato purée (paste)
1 x 400g [14oz] can chopped tomatoes
Italian seasoning, to taste
salt and pepper

Place a saucepan over a medium heat, then add the olive oil and garlic. Fry for 20–30 seconds until lightly golden (but not brown!). Add the tomato purée and fry for 30 seconds. Add the chopped tomatoes and a couple of pinches of Italian seasoning then simmer over a medium heat, stirring occasionally. After 5–10 minutes the sauce

should have reduced down and thickened. Season with salt and pepper to taste. Transfer to a bowl, cover with plastic wrap and chill in the fridge until ready to use.

Continued overleaf

1 / To make the dough, place the flour, salt and yeast together in a stand mixer fitted with a dough hook attachment (you can also use a bread machine just to knead). Make sure that the salt is not directly touching the yeast. Stir together, then pour in the water and olive oil.

Tip: If you don't have a machine for mixing the dough, or you have the time and want improved flavour and no need to knead, then simply mix all the ingredients together in a large bowl, cover with plastic wrap and leave the dough to rise overnight in the fridge until doubled in size. The second rise after shaping will take a little longer as the dough will still be cold from the fridge, but remember that the colder and slower the rise, the better the final Fat Cat Pizza will be!

2 / Place the dough in a lightly oiled large bowl, cover with oiled plastic wrap and leave to rise for about 1 hour or so (this depends on the ambient temperature – if the room is warmer, it will rise faster), or until doubled in size.

3 / Meanwhile, prepare the toppings for your pizza. At least 30 minutes before the dough is ready, preheat your oven to its maximum temperature to start preheating a baking steel, stone or simply a standard flat baking sheet (ideally one without a lip, for ease). Doing so will give your pizza a crispier base.

4 / When the dough has risen, set aside a little for the ears, then divide the remaining dough into 3 equal pieces, placing each piece onto an individual sheet of baking paper (scatter semolina on the paper first, if you like, to add extra crunch!). Use the heel of your hand to press each piece into a rough circle, then stretch the dough with your hand to thin it out, making the edges thicker than the middle. Use the reserved dough to add ears, pressing them very well to make sure they stick on.

5 / Add your toppings to the dough, leaving space at the top for the cat face. Add sliced black olives for the eyes and mouth.

6 / Leave the pizzas to prove at room temperature for about 20 minutes, or until puffed up slightly. They shouldn't increase much in size. If you did an overnight first rise, then just wait for the dough to come to room temperature (up to 2 hours) before you bake it.

7 / Once risen, slide any flat tray (or even a piece of stiff cardboard) under one of the pizzas – this should be easy to do as the pizza should be on a sheet of baking paper. Slide the pizza along with the baking paper onto the preheated stone, steel or baking sheet that's in the oven. If you're not using a heated tray, just simply place the tray of pizza in the oven as normal.

8 / Bake one pizza at a time, for around 5–12 minutes each. The hotter your oven and the hotter the baking stone or steel, the quicker they will bake!

9 / Once cooked, quickly paint the whiskers using black food dye mixed with a tiny amount of water and a paintbrush, then season with pepper, scatter with fresh basil (depending on your chosen toppings) and drizzle with extra olive oil. Serve straight away.

CAT TIP *"You don't choose us, we choose you! So your shaping might not go to plan, simply because that's the kitten that's chosen you and it's meant to be."*

The *Purrfect* Doughnut

You'll be a smitten kitten with these fluffy, light and proper doughnuts! As is often the case, it's essential you set aside at least one to snack on while decorating the others. You can also give these extra *purrsonality* if you're feline creative!

Try adding details using fondant, royal icing, coloured chocolate (use oil-based food dyes to avoid the chocolate seizing), or decorating some simply with cocoa powder paw prints – there are many *pawsibilities* beyond what is shown here!

Tip: You can fry these doughnuts without a deep-fryer (I've never owned one). Just use a deep pan filled with oil, and a thermometer that clips to the side. It helps to check the oil temperature and keep check of the frying times.

DIFFICULTY ❀ ❀ ❀ ❀ ❀

This is higher due to the handling of the dough, deep-frying and decorating. But if you're confident with any of those aspects, then you've got an advantage already.

MAKES: AROUND 12–14 RING DOUGHNUTS, AND 12–14 DOUGHNUT HOLES

Can be made vegan

DAIRY-BASED DOUGH (SEE VEGAN ALTERNATIVE ON PAGE 157)
375g [2⅔ cups] strong white flour
40g [¾ Tbsp] caster or granulated sugar
8g [½ Tbsp] salt
10g [⅓oz] instant fast-action dried yeast
finely grated zest of ½ orange
60ml [¼ cup] water
55ml [3⅔ Tbsp] whole milk
3 large eggs
80g [⅓ cup] unsalted butter, softened

TO DECORATE
24–28 whole blanched almonds (plus the same again if decorating all the kitten doughnut holes)
300g [10½oz] white chocolate (or vegan white chocolate), roughly chopped
various sprinkles (optional)
½ quantity of Royal Icing (see page 127) plus black food dye OR 50g [1¾oz] dark [semisweet] chocolate, melted

PLUS
vegetable oil, for oiling and deep-frying

> **Serving suggestion:** *You don't need to decorate ALL of these! Try decorating a few cats to be the focal points, then rolling the rest in caster or granulated sugar mixed with grated lemon zest. Serve with the plain doughnuts piled together, and the decorated ones on top. You can also make 3D Cookie Cats (page 12) or Fondant or Marzipan Cats (page 15) and sit these snugly inside some doughnut rings.*

Continued overleaf

1 / If working by hand, add the flour, sugar, salt, yeast and grated orange zest (if using) to a large bowl and stir for a few seconds to distribute the ingredients evenly.

2 / In a separate bowl, whisk the water, milk and eggs together. Add the liquid ingredients to the dry, and use a spoon to combine until you achieve a rough dough. Tip out the dough onto your work surface, and knead for 10–15 minutes until smooth and elastic. The dough will be sticky to start with, but avoid adding too much flour – it will gradually become less sticky as you knead it. If the dough sticks to the surface, use a dough scraper to scrape it off. Keep kneading until the dough is smooth; it will still be a little tacky but that is normal.

3 / Add the butter 40g [3 Tbsp] at a time and knead in. The dough may stick to the work surface but it is important to avoid adding any extra flour.

Tip: If you have a bread machine or stand mixer fitted with the dough attachment, simply add all the dry ingredients, mix, then add all the wet ingredients, except the butter. Let the machine knead the dough until smooth and elastic, about 7 minutes, then add the butter and let the machine knead this in for a further 5 minutes.

4 / Place the dough in a lightly oiled large bowl and cover with plastic wrap. Leave to rise until doubled in size, around 2–3 hours at room temperature.

Tip: If it's a cold day, you can speed up the rise by placing the covered dough in the oven preheated to no more than 30°C [86°F].

5 / When the dough has risen, knock it back and roll out on a lightly floured surface until about 2cm [¾in] thick. The dough will keep trying to shrink back every time you roll it out, so allow it to relax and shrink back a little. You can even walk away and come back to it after 10 minutes, to make it easier to roll to the desired thickness.

6 / Stamp out around 12–14 circles (I use an 8-cm [3¼-in] cutter) and carefully transfer each of these to an individual square of baking paper. Once transferred, you can cut out the centres (I use a 3-cm [1¼-in] cutter). Removing the centres after transferring to baking paper helps to make sure that each ring doughnut is even in size and shape.

7 / Reroll the dough to stamp out as many doughnuts as possible. Loosely cover the doughnuts with lightly oiled plastic wrap and leave to prove for 1–2 hours (depending on room temperature) until doubled in size.

8 / Heat enough oil for deep-frying in a large, deep pan to 180–185°C [350–365°F], and try to maintain this temperature while frying the doughnuts. Fry around 3 doughnuts at a time, carefully lowering them into the oil along with the baking paper underneath (this helps them to keep their shape and prevents deflation during transfer). Use tongs or a similar utensil to

remove the baking paper from the oil as quickly as possible. Fry the doughnuts for 45 seconds on each side. They should be deeply golden with a distinctive white ring around the sides (this is a good indicator that your doughnuts were proved for the right amount of time!)

9 / When the doughnuts have been fried on both sides, remove them from the oil with a slotted spoon and drain on paper towels. Leave to cool before decorating.

10 / To decorate, insert two of the almonds into the tops of each doughnut. Melt the white chocolate in the microwave using short 10–15-second bursts and stirring after each.

11 / Dip each doughnut face down into the white chocolate until coated, then place chocolate-side up on a baking sheet. Place sprinkles on the doughnuts now, if you like. Chill in the fridge for around 20 minutes to harden.

12 / Once hardened, you can add the details. You can either make royal icing, dyed black (page 129), or melt chocolate in 15–30-second bursts in the microwave, then transfer to a piping [pastry] bag, cut a small tip and use to pipe the details. If the chocolate is too runny, chill in the fridge for 1 minute. If it's too solid, microwave it for 5 seconds at a time. Add a sprinkle for the noses and sprinkles for the eyes, or pipe them on. Best eaten on the day they are made, or store in an airtight container for up to 3 days – a short blast in the microwave will soften them.

For the vegan dough:

TANGZHONG PASTE
100ml [⅓ cup plus 1 Tbsp] water
25g [2¾ Tbsp] strong white flour

VEGAN DOUGH
75ml [5 Tbsp] sunflower oil or
    neutral-tasting oil
2 Tbsp aquafaba
90ml [6 Tbsp] soy milk (or other
    plant-based milk)

40g [3¼ Tbsp] caster or granulated
    sugar
8g [½ Tbsp] salt
275g [2 cups] strong white flour, plus
    extra for dusting
12g [½oz] instant fast-action
    dried yeast

CAT TIP *"To make my unicorn horn, use the technique on page 32 (step 12) but make a mini version by cutting the cone smaller."*

1 / First, make the *tangzhong* paste. Using a balloon whisk, mix the water and flour together in a pan until smooth. Switch to a spatula and continue to stir until over a medium heat until thickened to a pudding-like consistency. Pour into a bowl, cover with plastic wrap (making sure it touches the surface of the *tangzhong*) and chill in the freezer for 10 minutes.

2 / Meanwhile, add the oil, aquafaba, soy milk, caster sugar and salt to a large bowl, or stand mixer if you have one. Add the chilled *tangzhong* to the bowl and whisk together (the oil will separate – this is normal and expected), then add the flour and yeast.

3 / Then follow the main recipe steps to knead the dough (skip the step where you add the butter), and continue as normal.

Purr-bread Cat Loaf

This is a how a cat would make a loaf of bread, if cats could bake. Simple and effortlessly cute... and there's absolutely no compromise on the finished product – it's soft on the inside and crusty (and cute!) on the outside. Just mix the ingredients together the evening before you want to bake it, then shape, score and bake in the morning. You'll get the best rise out of the bread when it hits the oven if you have a Dutch oven or cast-iron pan with a fitted lid. This will trap the steam and allow you to get a similar rise to a professional bread oven. But even without this, you can't really go wrong with this bread!

DIFFICULTY ❀ ❀

MAKES: 1 LOAF

Naturally vegan

500g [3½ cups] strong white flour, plus extra for dusting
2g [½ tsp] instant fast-action dried yeast

10g [2 tsp] fine salt
320ml [1⅓ cups] cold water
1 Tbsp olive oil
100g [1 cup] chopped olives (optional)

gel food dyes of your choice mixed with water (so the consistency is similar to watercolour paint)

1 / Add the flour to a large bowl. Add the yeast on one side and the salt on the other, then mix roughly using a spoon.

2 / Pour in the water and olive oil, then use a wooden spoon to mix into a rough ball, ensuring there is no dry flour remaining. Cover with oiled plastic wrap and leave overnight at room temperature.

3 / In the morning, line a bowl that's about the diameter/size you want the finished loaf to be with baking paper. Leave the paper poking out of the bowl so it's easy to pick up later. Pat the dough into a rough rectangle, then scatter the chopped olives on top and roll up, encasing the olives. Tuck the ends underneath and shape into a round with a smooth taut surface, with seams and creases underneath, using a little extra flour if needed. Try

to make sure that there aren't any olives popping out of the smooth surface – if any do, just pick them out. Place the dough, seam-side down, into the prepared bowl and leave to prove at room temperature until almost doubled in size – around 2 hours, although the exact time will depend on the ambient temperature.

4 / Meanwhile, preheat the oven to its maximum temperature. Preheat the Dutch oven or cast-iron pan for a good 45 minutes or so, if using, or a baking sheet if you don't have one.

5 / When the bread has finished its second rise, remove the Dutch oven (if using) from the oven and take off the lid – it will be extremely hot so make sure you use really good oven gloves! Lift the bread from the bowl, holding the paper like handles, then lower carefully

(along with the baking paper) into the Dutch oven, pot or onto the heated baking sheet. Dust the top of the loaf with 1 tsp of extra flour. Working quickly, paint a cat slightly to one side of the bread, using gel food dyes mixed with enough water to get it like watercolour paint (remember that colours will darken after baking). Using a very sharp knife or blade, score the dough lightly to create shadows, then deeply score to one side of the cat. Cover with the lid (if using), then place in the oven.

6 / Bake for 15 minutes at maximum temperature, then reduce to 220°C [425°F/Gas mark 7] and remove the lid (if using). Bake for a further 25 minutes – 40 minutes in total. Very carefully turn the bread out onto a wire rack and leave to cool. Store, wrapped in baking paper, cut-side down, for 2–3 days.

Tiger Loaf

The queen of the bread jungle: The Tiger Loaf. Slice open and use for extra fancy sandwiches, serve warm with soup, eat plain with lashings of butter... there are so many ways to eat this fun loaf with its extremely soft and fluffy insides. It's such a satisfying moment every time you cut a slice and see the swirls of tiger markings that are individual each and every time.

DIFFICULTY ❀ ❀ ❀

Can be made vegan

240ml [1 cup plus 1 tsp] tepid water
1½ tsp salt
1 Tbsp caster or granulated sugar
70g [⅓ cup minus 1 tsp] butter, melted (or vegan butter – use one that's close to 80% fat content)
400g [2¾ cups] strong white bread flour

MAKES: ONE 450-G [1-LB] LOAF

7g [2¼ tsp] instant fast-action dried yeast
orange and black gel food dyes (good-quality food dyes will really help you out)
1 Tbsp unsweetened cocoa powder (ideally, ultra Dutched black cocoa powder, as it's darker in colour, although any will do)
1 Tbsp hot water
neutral-tasting oil, for oiling

Continued overleaf

1 / To make the dough, add the tepid water, salt and sugar to a large bowl and mix until the salt and sugar have dissolved. Add the melted butter, then the flour and yeast and mix with a spoon until roughly mixed. Tip onto a work surface and use your hands to knead into a smooth, elastic ball of dough. You can use a little flour or oil to prevent sticking, but try to avoid using it. If the dough sticks to the work surface, use a dough scraper to easily remove it, but as you knead, it should become easier to handle. If you have a stand mixer or bread machine, then let the machine knead the dough for you.

2 / Divide the dough into 3 equal pieces. Add orange food dye to one piece and knead until it's orange throughout. Mix the cocoa powder with the hot water in a small bowl until smooth, then add this to a second piece of dough and knead in along with black food dye. The cocoa powder should help darken the base colour of the dough, so less black food dye needs to be added.

3 / Place the different pieces of dough into 3 separate lightly oiled bowls and cover with plastic wrap. Leave to rise until about doubled in size. The time this takes depends on the ambient temperature of the room, so if it's cold it will take longer, and if it's warm it will be faster.

4 / When risen, knock back and roll out each different coloured dough into a rectangle, about 10–12cm [4 –4½in] wide and 42cm [16½in] long. Use a little oil to prevent the dough sticking to the work surface.

Tip: The dough will try to resist being rolled and stretched back. If this happens, let it rest for 10 minutes then come back to it. It will roll with less resistance once the gluten has relaxed.

5 / Layer the orange rectangle on top of the black, then place the white rectangle on top. Cut this in half so that you have 2 smaller rectangles, then place one half on top of the other. Roll out again to the same size as previously, then repeat cutting it in half and placing one on top of the other.

6 / Lightly grease a 450-g [1-lb] loaf tin with butter. Shape the dough gently by tucking in the sides at the bottom so it looks like a neat loaf, with a smooth and taut top and any seams bunched underneath. Place in the prepared loaf tin and loosely cover with oiled plastic wrap. Leave to prove until the dough just reaches the top of the tin.

7 / Around 15 minutes or so before the bread has fully risen, preheat the oven to 220°C [425°F/Gas mark 7].

8 / Score the top of the loaf a few times using a very sharp knife or blade, then bake for 30 minutes, or until risen and browned on top. Eat fresh from the oven, or leave to cool first on a wire rack. Best eaten on the day it's made, or store in an airtight container for 4 days – this bread retains its softness well, but popping a slice in the toaster also helps to refresh it. Alternatively, freeze.

Fo-cat-ccia

Who knew that even the ordinary focaccia could get even better with daydreaming cats?

Your house will smell like comfort and coziness while this is baking, and you won't be able to resist tearing off a piece of soft, airy, freshly baked bread as soon as this is out of the oven. Focaccia isn't that hard to make either, as the overnight rise means you don't need to knead it AT ALL. The cute cat twist on the decoration is also an amazing way to use up leftover veggies in your fridge.

If you don't have time for an 18–26-hour overnight rise, you can leave the dough to rise for 1–2 hours at room temperature instead, but if you do this quicker option, then you WILL need to knead it, and the flavour won't be as well developed. It's also a very wet dough so you can't knead it like a lower-hydration dough, so it's easiest if you have a stand mixer with a dough hook attachment, or a bread machine, to do the kneading part. If you don't have any machines, I recommend you just plan ahead and go for the overnight rise!

DIFFICULTY 🐾 🐾
The actual focaccia is incredibly simple and requires no kneading (don't be daunted by the very wet dough – you don't have to handle it much at all), then it's just down to you to put the cat in the fo-cat-cia, which can be as simple or as elaborate as you like.

MAKES: 1 SHARING-SIZED 23 X 33-CM [9 X 13-IN] FLATBREAD

Can be made vegan

500g [3½ cups] strong white flour, plus extra for dusting
2 tsp fine salt
7g [2¼ tsp] instant fast-action dried yeast
450ml [2 cups] lukewarm water
4 Tbsp olive oil, plus extra for oiling and to serve
butter or margarine (can be vegan), for greasing
1 tsp flaky sea salt

TO DECORATE
your choice of vegetables to create a cat scene! Use a knife or peeler to remove the courgette [zucchini] skin, and cut this and arrange to form the cat design. Other useful toppings are fresh rosemary, halved cherry tomatoes, sliced radishes, and carrots (which you can cut into fish shapes), but you can use anything you have in the fridge to create unique designs! Get your thinking cat on!

Continued overleaf

CAT TIP *Calling all garlic lovers! You can roast some garlic and squeeze this into your dough. Preheat the oven to 200°C [400°F/Gas mark 6]. Cut 5mm–1cm [¼–½in] from the tops of 2 whole bulbs of garlic to expose the individual cloves. Place these on a square of foil, then drizzle 1 Tbsp of olive oil over each exposed head and wrap the whole bulb completely in the foil. Roast for 30–40 minutes, then once cool enough to handle, squeeze out the soft garlic and mix it randomly into the dough after its first rise.*

1 / Place the flour, fine salt and yeast in a large bowl. Make sure that the salt is not directly touching the yeast. Stir together, then pour in the water and mix with a spoon or spatula to create a sticky dough.

2 / Rub the surface of the dough with 1 Tbsp of the olive oil to prevent it drying out and/or sticking to the plastic wrap. Cover the bowl with plastic wrap and place in the fridge for 18–26 hours.

3 / When the dough has risen to more than double its size, remove it from the fridge and use oiled fingers to gently ease it out of the bowl and onto an oiled surface to prevent it sticking. Pick up one side and fold it to the centre, then repeat with all the other sides to create a rough parcel shape. If you're adding the extra roasted garlic (see the box above), then flatten the dough out with your hands, distribute the garlic all over and fold the dough up.

4 / Turn the dough over and coat it generously all over with another tablespoon of the olive oil. Place it in a lightly buttered 23 x 33-cm [9 x 13-in] shallow rectangular tin and leave to rise at room temperature for 2–4 hours. It will spread out and gradually fill the tin.

Tip: While the dough is rising, prepare the toppings for your design later – just lay out the design on your surface, so you can quickly transfer it to the risen focaccia later. The toppings shrink a small amount when baking, so cut them slightly bigger than you want the end result to look.

5 / When the focaccia has risen, preheat the oven to 220°C [425°F/Gas mark 6]. Drizzle with the remaining 2 Tbsp olive oil, then press your fingers firmly into the dough to make deep dimples all over. You can be very firm with it! Sprinkle over the flaky salt.

6 / Decorate with your chosen cut vegetables to create a cute picture, then press more dimples in around the vegetables, if they have risen while creating the picture.

7 / Bake for 20–25 minutes until golden.

8 / Once cooked and still hot, drizzle with more olive oil, then serve hot or turn out and leave to cool on a wire rack, then serve with extra olive oil as desired.

Kitten Buns in Flowerpots

Where have those kittens got to now? What? They're in the flowerpots? You've got to be kitten me.

Fur-real though, why do cats love sitting in plant pots so much? Whatever the reason, in honour of this cat quirk, this is a recipe for the softest, fluffiest bread you can find, and that is all thanks to the *tangzhong* technique. *Tangzhong* is simply a roux made with flour and water, which is then cooled and added to the dough mixture. This roux essentially locks in the liquid and helps to give the final bread a higher moisture content. The resulting bread is soft, cloud-like and stays fresher for longer. Making the roux takes 5 minutes of your time, but completely transforms this bread.

DIFFICULTY 🐾 🐾 🐾
The actual dough is *meownimal* effort to make. The trickiest aspect is knowing when the bread has proved but isn't under- or overproved! The colder your room, the slower these will rise. And on a hot day, the first cats you assemble might be fully risen by the time you finish with the last, so you might need to bake them in stages. If in doubt, it's better to bake a slightly underproved dough, than an overproved one. You'll know it's overproved if you poke it lightly and it sinks down without bouncing back up at all.

MAKES: 9–12 (DEPENDING ON SIZE OF FLOWERPOTS)

Can be made vegan

TANGZHONG PASTE
100ml [⅓ cup plus 1 Tbsp] water
25g [2¾ Tbsp] strong white flour

DOUGH
125ml [½ cup] whole milk (or any plant-based milk)
30g [2 Tbsp] unsalted butter (or vegan butter – use one that's close to 80% fat content)
sunflower or other neutral-tasting oil, for oiling
10g [2½ tsp] caster or granulated sugar
1 tsp salt
1 large egg (or replace with 30ml [2 Tbsp] vegetable oil and 30ml [2 Tbsp] plant-based milk)

350g [2½ cups] strong white flour, plus extra for dusting
7g [2¼ tsp] instant fast-action dried yeast

PLUS
1 egg, to brush on top before baking (or use 4 parts plant-based milk to 1 part golden [light corn] syrup, or any other liquid sugar, such as maple syrup)

TO DECORATE
edible black ink pen, or black food dye mixed with a small amount of water
small quantity of Royal Icing (page 127) and different gel food dyes
edible flowers

Continued overleaf

1 / First, make the *tangzhong* paste. Using a balloon whisk, mix the water and flour together in a pan until smooth. Place the pan over a medium heat and stir constantly with a spatula until thickened to a pudding-like consistency. Pour into a bowl, cover with plastic wrap (making sure it touches the surface of the *tangzhong*) and chill in the freezer for 10 minutes.

2 / Meanwhile, for the dough, gently warm up the milk in the microwave – it should be warm but not hot. Melt the butter in the microwave. Lightly oil a large bowl.

3 / Place the milk and butter in another large bowl and add the sugar and salt. Add the chilled *tangzhong* along with the egg (or oil and milk mixture) and whisk together with a balloon whisk.

4 / Add the flour and yeast to the mixture. If using a stand mixer, just allow the machine to knead for 10 minutes with the dough hook attachment. If working by hand, use a wooden spoon to combine everything into a shaggy ball of dough, then turn out onto a floured work surface and knead by hand for about 10–15 minutes. The dough will be sticky to start with, but avoid adding too much flour – it will

gradually become less sticky as you knead it. If the dough sticks to the surface, use a dough scraper to scrape it off. Keep kneading until the dough is smooth; it will still be a little tacky but this is normal.

5 / Place the dough in the oiled large bowl and cover with plastic wrap. Leave to rise at room temperature until about doubled in size. This takes about 1 hour, but can vary significantly depending on the ambient temperature of where you leave it.

6 / When the dough has doubled in size, turn it out onto a lightly floured work surface and knock back. Pinch off a small amount of the dough (for the ears) and set aside. Then divide the remaining dough into 9–12 balls, depending on the size of your flowerpots. Shape by tucking the dough under and pinching at the bottom to create a smooth taut top surface.

7 / Place the dough balls in silicone flowerpots (or anything else ovenproof with a similar shape). These should only fill just over a third of the container, as they will double in size when rising then significantly increase in size again when baking due to oven spring. They will ultimately become about three times their original size.

8 / Shape small balls of the remaining dough into ears for the cats and stick them on firmly.

9 / Cover with lightly oiled plastic wrap and leave to prove until about doubled in size. The time this takes varies depending on the temperature of the location, but won't be as long as the first rise. You are looking for the dough to nearly double in size and should spring back halfway when lightly indented with a finger. Fifteen minutes before the end of the rise, preheat the oven to 180°C [350°F/Gas mark 4].

10 / Whisk the egg (or the plant-based milk mixed with golden syrup) in a small bowl, then brush this on top of the dough and bake for 15 minutes, or until risen and lightly golden brown.

11 / Leave the flowerpot cats to completely cool on a wire rack, then add cute facial features with an edible black pen, or with black food dye mixed with the tiniest amount of water. Or make a small batch of Royal Icing following the instructions on page 129 and dye this different colours, then pipe on faces and simple little icing flowers. Top with an edible flower (or several) on top of the cats' heads.

CAT TIP *"Ensure you attach my ears firmly, otherwise they can fall off. Squeeze the extra ball of dough on with your fingers to firmly attach it, and THEN press this into an ear shape..."*

"...But you can always hide any misshapen ears with flowers..."

- INDEX -

Acknowledgements

It feels like the idea for this book has been floating in my brain since forever, and I'm so overwhelmed with happiness that it finally exists in physical form. Those of you who made this a reality know who you are, and I want you to know how much I massively appreciate your help, advice and support. I couldn't have done it without you. There are also many more of you who may *not* know who you are, but you have also contributed to this book being what it is – because the reason this book is here is a collection of loads of small fragments of support, kindness and community. Maybe I was having a bad day and you randomly said something nice to me. Maybe you inspired an idea, directly or indirectly. Maybe you have helped a cat, therefore growing the love for cats in the world.

This book wouldn't exist without you all and your love for baking, kindness and cats. You've all helped it become what it is, and this book has a piece of many of you in it, whether you know it or not. Thank you.

And of course – thank you to my boys, my feline family, my sidekicks in life: Inki, Mochi and Nabil. I'm also forever grateful to all the cats of this world for being constant sources of joy, weirdness and inspiration.

Perhaps most importantly, thank you to those of you who have ever done something kind for a cat in any way. Keep spreading the happiness in this world.

MANAGING DIRECTOR: Sarah Lavelle
COMMISSIONING EDITOR: Harriet Webster
ASSISTANT EDITOR: Sofie Shearman
DESIGNER: Alicia House
PHOTOGRAPHER: Ellis Parrinder
ILLUSTRATOR: Linda van den Berg
LETTERING: Mary Kate McDevitt
FOOD STYLIST: Kim-Joy
ASSISTANT FOOD STYLIST: Sarah Hardy
PROP STYLIST: Charlotte Barber
HAIR & MAKE-UP: Thembi Mkandla
HEAD OF PRODUCTION: Stephen Lang
SENIOR PRODUCTION CONTROLLER:
Sabeena Atchia

Published in 2023 by Quadrille,
an imprint of Hardie Grant Publishing

QUADRILLE
52–54 Southwark Street
London SE1 1UN
quadrille.com

Cataloguing in Publication Data: a catalogue
record for this book is available from the British
Library.

Text © Kim-Joy 2023
Photography © Ellis Parrinder 2023
Design and layouts © Quadrille 2023

Reprinted in 2023 (thrice)
10 9 8 7 6 5 4

ISBN 978 1 78713 941 1

Printed in China

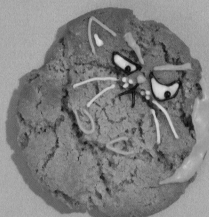

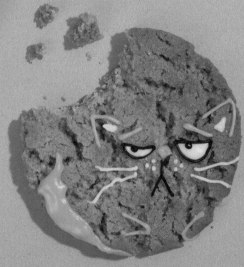